THE IRISH FUTURE

AND

THE LORDSHIP OF THE WORLD

THE IRISH FUTURE

Charles J. O'Donnell, of Carndonagh, County Donegal,
M.P. Walworth, London, 1906-10

THE IRISH FUTURE

AND

THE LORDSHIP OF THE WORLD

BY

C. J. O'DONNELL

Ex-M.P., LONDON

" Things are being done in Ireland that would disgrace the blackest annals of the lowest despotism in Europe."— Mr. H. Asquith (Earl of Oxford), in 1921.

" In the Great War one battalion alone lost one hundred and eighty officers and over four thousand rank and file."— *The Passing of the Munsters, The Times,* 9th June, 1922.

" For we wrestle not against flesh and blood but against principalities and powers, against the rulers of the darkness of this world, against the spirit of wickedness in high places.

" Stand, therefore, having your loins girt about with truth and your feet shod with the preparation of the gospel of peace."—*St. Paul to the Ephesians,* Chap. vi. 12-15.

CECIL PALMER
FORTY-NINE
CHANDOS
STREET
W.C.2

Price five shillings net

FIRST EDITION JANUARY 1929
SECOND EDITION JANUARY 1930
C O P Y R I G H T

Made and Printed in Great Britain at the KEMP HALL PRESS
in the City of Oxford

A FEW OPINIONS OF THE PRESS
on the First Edition (1924) of
THE LORDSHIP OF THE WORLD

The Times.—" Mr. O'Donnell is a trenchant writer, able to put his case clearly and forcibly and to back it up by the apt use of facts and documents, but most readers will find much to criticize in it, though they will be stimulated by its strong and original individuality and its store of information. . . . He does not at all like the Irish Treaty, partly because of the Partition, but also because it renders Ireland powerless and isolated, her natural home being within the British Empire, which is in his view essentially a Celtic Empire. . . . He devotes many pages to America, which he knows well but strongly criticizes, especially its ' Kuklux Orangeism,' and he magnifies the work accomplished there by the Irish race. . . . He defends Germany vigorously against charges of inhumanity, atrocities, and useless destruction."

The Northern Whig, *of Belfast, The Organ of Protestant Ulster.*—" This is perhaps the most original book yet written about the Great War."

The Saturday Review.—" Mr. O'Donnell is forceful and has a world policy to set forth in a manner that shall seize and hold."

Right Hon. Sir Gilbert Parker, P.C.—" Its very plain and powerful pages are a very useful contribution to the political literature of our times."

The Honble. W. E. Borah, *Chairman of the Committee on Foreign Affairs, United States Senate.*—" I am intensely interested and thoroughly enjoyed reading your book. I find the chapters contain information which I have been anxious to gather in some systematic form. And it is not only the information contained but it is the lucid, incisive presentation as well, which interests me."

Mr. Arnold White.—" Never have I read a book with a more intensive atmosphere of honesty."

His Eminence Cardinal Logue. —" A most just book. I could not put it down."

Right Hon. Viscount Morley of Blackburn.—" I read with care and keen interest the pamphlet (Chapters on Ireland) you are kind enough to send me. It abounds in excellent and vital things, finely set forth."

Jerome K. Jerome.—" Thank God! Someone has arisen to tell the truth."

The Tablet, *The Leading Catholic Journal.*—" Mr. C. J. O'Donnell, that well-known Catholic Irishman, whose brother, Frank Hugh O'Donnell, was such a power in Nationalist politics, has just published a book which makes you feel as if you have picked up a hedgehog. It bristles in every paragraph with contentious comments, opinions, predictions and declarations. . . . He has no use for the Asquithian Liberals. . . . On American and especially Irish-American life and politics there are some remarkable chapters."

The Court Journal.—" In his introduction Mr. O'Donnell makes a strong pronouncement in favour of the foreign policy of Lord Salisbury, as against the policy which has been pursued since his day. Perhaps the most interesting chapter of the book is that entitled ' The Anglo-Saxon Myth,' in which he states the case for what may be termed the Celtic origin of the British Empire."

The Newcastle Chronicle.—" Mr. O'Donnell's book is a vigorous onslaught on Liberal statesmanship and the ' Irish jelly fish ' in Parliament."

Kansas City Press.—" An absorbing book."

Daily News.—" An extremely readable piece of political writing."

Opinions on German Translation

The Kölnische Zeitung.—" He has rendered a great service to the cause of peace, and it is much to be desired that the book should be widely circulated throughout the Anglo-Saxon world and especially in the United States."

The Morgenpost *of Berlin.*—" He denounces the failure of Liberal Policy in England, which was catastrophic, as it brought the country in line with France instead of with the German Reich, the natural friend of England."

The Neueste Nachrichten *of Vienna.*—" He is almost as sarcastic as Shaw himself when he comes to speak of the ' systematic poisoning ' of public opinion, which was called ' Truth '."

The Tageblatt *of Weisbaden.*—"He refutes most brilliantly the many stupid but generally believed stories about German barbarities."

The Reichspost *of Hamburg.*—" In strongly substantiated statements he gives us some illuminating facts regarding the fateful rôles of the Prime Minister (Asquith) and the Foreign Secretary (Grey), on whom he lays the blame of the greatest calamity that Europe has ever experienced."

BY THE SAME AUTHOR

THE FAILURE OF
LORD CURZON

THIRD EDITION

Opinions of the Press.

(i.) THE SPEAKER.—" The writer's statements are concise, his style bright and racy, and those who do not desire to live in a fool's paradise should read his vigorous exposition of the methods by which the fabric of our Indian Empire is being undermined."

(ii.) THE CONTEMPORARY REVIEW.—" There is no lack of knowledge in this uncompromising indictment. . . . Whether we agree with the author or not, his book is worth reading as an exposition of an honest though unpopular view of Indian administration, written by one who has given the greater part of his life to the work."

(iii.) THE ATHENÆUM.—" A healthy counterstroke to official optimism. . . . The *whole* book should be read by all interested in Indian administration."

(iv.) LIVERPOOL POST.—" A trenchant yet courteous criticism."

(v.) LIBERTY REVIEW.—" The array of facts and the opinions of distinguished statesmen and administrators, collected in the book, forcibly arrests one's attention."

THE CAUSES OF PRESENT
DISCONTENTS IN INDIA

FOURTH EDITION

7

Dedication

To the Peace-Seeking Members of Parliament of
All Parties

Gentlemen,

In dedicating this volume to you I would
remind you that the Prime Minister of England
has done a great work of peace not only in
America but in Europe by denouncing the flagrant injustice done to minority populations by
the War Treaties. His warning, however, that
" unless the minority problems are solved in a
spirit of mutual respect and of give-and-take
there will be grave trouble," applies to Northern
Ireland more closely than to any other part of
Europe, and we should keep our own breath
to cool our own porridge. The condition of
things in Ulster is intolerable, and its Catholic
inhabitants, numbering 420,426 out of a total
population of 1,256,561 are, according to an
authoritative statement by the Catholic Bishops
of Ulster, systematically wronged by the Orange
Parliament at Belfast with the connivance and
even the pecuniary subvention of the late Conservative Government. " The utter disregard of
the rights of Catholics, this ever-advancing

9

aggression on Catholics, is a grave menace to the peace of the whole community, and we consider the time has come for our people to organise openly on constitutional lines and resolve to lie down no longer under this *degrading thraldom.*"

That was a few years ago, but there has been absolutely no improvement. In fact, things are appreciably worse. The latest outrage has been the withdrawal of the right of Proportionate Representation, which was an integral part of the settlement of 1922, and which, to my mind, could be repealed only by the Imperial Parliament, with the consent of the second party to the pact, viz. : the Catholic minority. It should be noted that this action was also most injurious to the Labour Party, a very numerous body in Belfast.

Mr. Joseph Devlin, M.P., in August of last year, 1928, said, " After waiting for seven years,—years of justice denied, disabilities imposed, and religious and political inferiority branded upon our people,—we are still treated as pariahs and outcasts in the community, in which we are citizens." There is not much " mutual respect and give-and-take " in this precious state of things. How much more money will the British Exchequer pay to Belfast in order to maintain Orange bigotry ? It is folly to talk of a permanent settlement of the Irish Question so long as this idiotic religious enmity is fed and fostered by Englishmen of light and leading. Truly did Burke say " Magnanimity in politics is not seldom the truest wisdom and a great empire and little minds go ill together."

Dedication

Gentlemen, an admirable effort is being made to improve relations with the United States of America, a design which this book seeks to support strongly. Nothing will or can hamper goodwill so much as the " Anglo-Saxon " policy of the Quota, which must make the very name of Englishman offensive to nearly every other race, to Irish and German, to Italian and Pole, to Swede and Jew. Under its fantastic Nordic nonsense the Orange Earl O'Neil from Belfast is a desirable citizen and Cardinal O'Donnell from Donegal a racial degenerate. I wonder under what category Mr. Henry Ford from Cork and Mr. Andrew Mellon from Wexford find their places. Mr. Kellogg is, I believe, from Southern Ireland. The fact is that this wrong to citizenship is a Ku-Klux-Klan device, religious not racial, as pointed out by Mr. J. L. Garvin in the *Observer* of 27th January, 1924. The Press of London generally expressed goodwill towards this foolish and dangerous manœuvre and failed to appreciate the irritation and anger that must result. It binds together every race in the States in a common hostility against British influence. This anti-English feeling, deplorable from every standpoint, will continue, under Irish Catholic guidance, so long as on both sides of the Atlantic, in Ulster, the U.S.A., and Canada, the folly of the bigot is allowed to usurp the rôle of the statesman.

A peculiarly base slander against Ireland has been propagated, mostly in America, during the past decade, alleging that her manhood failed the

Dedication

Allies in the Great War. As shown in Chapter IV the facts are overwhelmingly the other way. I may summarise them in the words of the Right Honble Lord Glenavy, the President of the Senate in Dublin and the most distinguished Protestant in the Free State. Speaking last year at Trinity College, of which he is Vice-Chancellor, he said " Of Ireland's whole population about 1,000,000 were fitted by age and physique for active service and of these *at least* 400,000 or more than one in every three were numbered in the fighting forces on land and sea." Lord Kitchener said they were " magnificent." In proportion to population no nationality in the British Empire sent so many recruits in the first three months of the War as Ireland, and they were rewarded, in the terrible phrase of Mr. Lloyd George, by " malignant " ill-usage and insults. The Irish in America claim that a third of the vast army that crossed the Atlantic to England's help were of Irish origin.

I solicit also your most serious consideration of the Chapter XIII entitled " The Supreme Question of India," and I say with the most complete sincerity and knowledge that the Indian people are singularly loyal to the King-Emperor and the British connection, but that does not prevent a discontent, amounting almost to sedition, and with good cause. The greatest danger in the future, it may be the near future, is a rising of the Indian peasantry, possibly in every province, against the Land Tax. The time will then have arrived when the warning given by that sympathetic Irishman, Lord

Dedication

Lawrence, the greatest of Indian Viceroys, in the House of Lords some seventy years ago will be fulfilled and the British power will sink, overwhelmed by the anger of India's agricultural millions.

In fine, I beg your perusal of Chapter XIV, "The Celtic Empire of Great Britain." It is time that the supremacy of the Celt, of the Briton, the Scot, and the Irishman should be recognised. The Teutonic or Saxon element in the English homeland is small, as all the greatest students of ethnography, Huxley, Boyd-Dawkins, and Beddoe, have incontestably proved. In the words of Professor A. H. Sayce, Queen's College, Oxford, "The anthropological evidence of the Celtic origin of the people of England is clear. The archæological evidence is also definite. The Anglo-Saxon myth is very nearly dead" amongst educated people. The predecessors of the Prime Minister from Bute and Aberdeen to Gladstone, Balfour, Campbell-Bannerman, Lloyd George, and Bonar Law, were Celts, mostly Scotch, as were Brougham and Palmerston. Pitt and Peel, Raleigh and Drake, were, like Russell and Cavendish, British Celts from the Welsh borderland. The Stuarts were Celts. The Tudors (Theodores) and Cecils (Cyselts) were Welsh, as was Cromwell (Williams). Ireland gave to the Empire the immortal Edmund Burke, Canning and Sheridan, and nearly all our great generals, except Marlborough (out of Cornwall), from Wellington to Roberts.

The great generals of the Great War, French and Haig, were Celts and so were the great Admirals,

13

Dedication

Jellicoe (from Cornwall), and the three Irishmen,—Beatty, Madden, and the forgotten O'Callaghan, of whom Earl Jellicoe said in 1914, " Sir George Callaghan had trained the (Channel) command to a pitch of perfection no fleet had ever attained before." *That was the fleet that saved England.*

The Scotch in thousands have pushed our trade into every corner of the globe and made it the wonderful thing we know, whilst Irish soldiers have done far more than their share in bringing into being the greatest empire in the world. India was the great prize of a Gaelic-speaking army, recruited by the East India Company exclusively in Ireland, under Irish generals, Gough, Keane, Wellington, and Coote. The same ancient speech was used by the glorious Scotch regiments down to the time of the Crimean War. The makers of Canada were, nearly all, Scotchmen, headed by Lords Strathcona and Mount Stephen, helped by another Celt, Lord O'Shaugnessy. The makers of Australia were mostly Irish. Only one thing is needed, and that is the recognition of the ethnological fact that the British are mainly a Celtic race, which, like the Irish, survived all the conquests, Roman, Saxon, and Norman, the chief member of a Celtic Partnership. I refer to this question at some length, because it bears in its future a great peace-making influence.

Yours very truly,

C. J. O'DONNELL.

50 *Hans Crescent, S.W.*1.
9*th October,* 1929

Introduction

(i) " Absolutely the most important thing in this world
at the present time is to maintain a good and permanent
understanding between the British Empire and the Republic of North America. Ireland stands between these
great Powers, both geographically and politically. It
may be her destiny, having won freedom for herself,
'from the centre to the sea,' to bind these two mighty
nations into a peaceful and peace-giving world power.
Over a century ago the great Irish orator and statesman,
Henry Grattan, warned England that what 'you trample
on in Ireland will sting you in America.' "

*The Lordship of the
World*, page 146.

(ii) " Until we realise that the Irish question is an
American question we shall miss its capital meaning.
The United States is concerned about it because it is the
most vital of its domestic issues. The man with a conviction, said Stuart Mill, is more powerful than ninety-
nine who have only interests. But the Irish are not one
in a hundred. They are at least one in ten. They move
as a vehement stream through the confused and tumultuous
life of the nation. They permeate the whole structure of
society. They are powerful in finance, in law, in literature, in the services."
" Consider the facts. The Irish form the most solid
and formidable political mass in the country. They
are formidable, not so much because of their great

15

Introduction

numbers, as because they are the one political body moving with a single idea in a compact mass through the life of the nation. They are not socially negligible. They are in the Seats of the Mighty."

"The most brilliant writers on the Press are Irish. Nearly every political caucus is under Irish control. Most of the great cities have Irish mayors. The police are almost invariably Irish. The Irish vote is the crucial element of every election. No candidate, whether for a mayorality, a State Governorship, the Senate, or the Presidency, can ignore it."

The Anglo-American Future,
by Mr. A. G. Gardiner.

THERE was a great improvement in Irish-American feeling after the Irish Treaty with Great Britain in 1922, but all that has been undone by the gross ill-usage of Ulster Catholics by the Belfast Parliament and the "Anglo-Saxon" blow at Southern Ireland by the "Quota Policy" at Washington.

This volume is in large part a development of the arguments in *The Lordship of the World,* published in 1924. Since then the World

Irish Influence.
has moved far and, as an Irishman, I am chiefly interested in the wonderful expansion of Irish influence in recent years. Many nations have come to life again since the War, but none has had opened out before it a more world-wide and promising future. A quarter of the twentieth century passed away amid the cataclysmic events of the Great War and preparation for it. The beginning of the second

quarter finds Ireland in the most pregnant period of her very chequered existence. She has, to her great satisfaction, two most notable events to record:

(i) The full recognition of her claim to nation-hood by the civilised nations of the World at Geneva, and (ii) the definite accession of her friend, the United States of America, to the hegemony of a very large part of the World, West and East.

Considering that two-thirds of the Irish people, some twenty millions of, physically and mentally, a very vigorous race, now find their homes in North America and may become in a few years the most powerful force in its public life, the dominant influence of the United States in world politics, trade, and finance is a fact of supreme importance to Ireland.

Ireland is no doubt now a free nation, but no effort is being made by any English Party or by the English people as a whole to help her in her labour, and if she **The Quota Outrage.** is to remain a part and a very important part of the Empire she must be conciliated whole-heartedly. Ireland has been broken in pieces and then thrown on the scrap-heap. Can this be a permanent settlement? The outrage inflicted by the Quota legislation at Washington, under which the vast body of Irish immigrants is insolently divided, according to Orange doctrine, into Northern and Southern, Protestant and Catholic, makes for trouble. That this outrage should be inflicted on the Irish race at the very outset of its existence as a recognised nation

is a noticeable fact. It is bad enough that Irish
Catholics should be harassed and cheated out
of their rights as citizens in Orange Ulster, but
that the anti-Catholic mania should extend to
Washington is an unbearable state of things, and
justifies very vigorous action by the Catholics of
the United States. The attack has been utterly
without provocation and means that the majority
of the Senate and of the Congress and the Government of the United States are hostile to and eager
to injure one of the largest sections of its population.

I am writing as one, who, through a long life
passed mostly in the service of the British Crown,
has been firmly and honestly con-
A Helot Condition. vinced that it was within the British
Empire that the Irish nation should
find her most promising home. In India I had
learned how great a power for good that empire
could be, in spite of some grievous errors. My
belief and my hope have been seriously undermined by my observations since my return from
India in 1900 and especially by my experiences as a
Member of Parliament for a London constituency. I found that, whilst the mass of the people
of England, Scotland, and Wales were sincere
well-wishers of Ireland, the upper classes, so
powerful in politics, were hostile to every just
demand of Irish opinion. I found that, whilst
the Conservatives were openly advocates of re-
pression, the seeming goodwill of the Liberals
was mostly, at least in their higher ranks, vote-
seeking lip-service. In the following pages there

18

Introduction

is a chapter on Ulster and Partition, to which I hope
my readers will give more than a passing notice.
The chief object of this book is to call on Irishmen the world over to take all necessary measures
to rescue the Catholics of Ulster, of whom I am
one, from " a degrading thraldom," as the Catholic
Bishops of Ulster, in convention assembled, defined
the present helot condition of its Catholic inhabitants.

I also describe the war services of Irishmen and
the black ingratitude with which they were rewarded, and it is to be noted that
it was under a Liberal Government,
with Mr. Asquith at its head, that
these follies were committed, whilst it was under
the Premiership of Mr. Lloyd George that the
Black and Tans were let loose on Southern Ireland.
Mr. Asquith seemed to me intellectually anti-
Irish, anti-Catholic, and, I am inclined to think,
anti-Liberal, though the exigencies of politics drove
him in the opposite directions. He had for years
been living in the degenerate atmosphere of " The
Souls "[1] and in it lost his own political soul. His

Black Ingratitude.

---

[1] The following description of one of the best of them, a
brave and brilliant young man, under the semi-pagan influence
of the " Souls " makes painful reading, " Raymond Asquith
—killed in battle 14th September, 1916—was intellectually
one of the most distinguished young men of his day and
beautiful to look at, added to which he was light in hand,
brilliant in answer, and interested in affairs. When he went to
Balliol he cultivated a kind of cynicism which was an endless
source of delight to the young people around him ; in a good-
humoured way he made a butt of God and smiled at man."—
Autobiography of Margot Asquith. And this is our *Kultur.*

19

Introduction

ambition seemed to be to conciliate Conservative opinion and, where he was accepted, to move in Conservative circles. I am far from blaming the strong Conservative tendencies of his character, quite the other way, but he was entirely incapable of evolving a measure of self-government that would satisfy an Irish Nationalist. He would give the least possible and take the longest time possible in giving it. I think he had an inborn Anglo-Saxon hostility to the Celt, and his relations with his Welsh successor probably did not inclined him to a more pronounced affection. The free hand he knowingly,—I say knowingly, because he was fully warned,—gave to the War Office in its anti-Irish manœuvres in 1914 was only a part of his really anti-Irish sentiments. His natural partner was Sir Edward Carson, whom he soon called to his Cabinet. It was Mr. Asquith who, in order to placate his Orange master, invented the Policy of Partition and the segregation of North Eastern Ulster, a policy unknown to Mr. Gladstone, to Sir Henry Campbell-Bannerman, and even to Lord Rosebery. He more than condoned the Curragh Mutiny in spite of Lord French's advice. So far as permanent results go he was more mischievous than Sir Edward Carson, an honest and able man, who loathed Home Rule, though his father stood beside Isaac Butt at the Rotondo in Dublin when that policy was launched in 1873. Mr. Asquith indoctrinated[1]

[1] He seems to have indoctrinated his own household with a similar virus. Mrs. Asquith in the second volume of her

20

Introduction

the Liberal Party with his procrastinating methods
in regard to Ireland, which ultimately destroyed
Home Rule and with it helped to sweep himself
and his followers out of power, probably for ever,
—a weakling but, unhappily, in power in 1914.
At the very outset of the War, Mr. Asquith
showed the anti-Irish trend of his mind by per-
mitting Mr. Churchill to dismiss from
his command the distinguished Irish   **An Irish Admiral.**
Admiral, Sir George Callaghan. Earl
Jellicoe said it was one of " the saddest moments
in his life," when, " on August 3, 1914, he had
to board the flagship and tell Sir George Callaghan, his late chief, that he had come to
take over the command which Sir George had
trained to a pitch of perfection no fleet had ever
attained before." In his *World Crisis,* page 218,
Mr. Churchill makes the admission that " It was
naturally a cruel blow to Sir George Callaghan
to have to lay down his charge at such a moment,
and his protests were re-echoed by practically
all the principal admirals who had served under
him and by Sir John Jellicoe himself. It was
also a grave matter to make a change in the com-

Autobiography gives us the following Liberal appreciation of
the Irish character : " Celtic blood is usually accompanied
by excited brains and a reckless temperament, and is always
an excuse for exaggeration. When not whining or wheedling,
the Celt is usually in a state of bluff or funk, and can always
wind himself up to the kind of rhetoric that no housemaid
can resist." Contempt rather than anger is the proper reply to
such language, but even that treatment does not help towards
good will. The lady is a Celt, of the Anglo-Saxon species,

21

mand of the fleets at this juncture." It was a shameful business and everyone knew that the real meaning of it was that Churchill feared to find in the strong Irishman a less obedient servant in his interferences in strictly naval matters. For instance his order to mobilize the fleet without the consent of the Cabinet was possible only when dealing with complaisant Sea Lords. There is nothing to show that Admiral Callaghan was too old, but, if this were so, he ought to have had an adequate reward, at least a peerage. He was degraded for his protests. During the first few months of the War the Admiralty did not distinguish itself.

I may state that I have a second object in writing this book; that is, to implore wealthy **Education the** Irishmen, especially in the United **Supreme Need.** States, to give out of their superabundant riches large endowments to Irish education. I must confess that, like most of my educated fellow countrymen, I have in the past been horrified or disgusted by crimes and idiotic policies in Free State Ireland, but they were the work and the ideals of the enemies of the Irish Government. I have faith in my people and believe that such degradation is now due to the want of education. There is no country in the civilised world that has such an undeveloped system of education, higher, middle, and primary. Her universities are poverty-stricken and the rewards of the professorial career are pitiably meagre. It is a common complaint that the

Introduction

Catholic Church and especially the Jesuit Order
hold too strong a position in the National University, but we owe them a deep gratitude for
much excellent and almost unpaid work. There
are no funds to employ lay professors of distinction.

It is the want of education that has so often
placed Irish politicians in an undesirable position.
At the beginning of the Great War they were
the victims of anti-German propa-
ganda, of fables, which were believed. **Anti-German Propaganda.**
no matter how absurd. Thus Mr,
John Redmond thundered against the German
soldiery, very largely Catholic, telling the people
of Waterford in December, 1914, that " the Boches
were hunting priests and nuns and wantonly destroying Catholic Churches." He never learned,
I dare say, that in an interview granted in 1915
to M. Latapie, the correspondent of the Paris
Liberté, Pope Benedict XV stated in regard to
the charge of ill-usage of priests in Belgium, a
very favourite falsehood in Catholic countries,
that " The Cardinal Secretary has received reports from seven Belgian congregations," Domini-
cans, Jesuits, Franciscans, and others, " that they
had not a single case to bring forward."

I cannot believe that the very crude ideals of
Mr. de Valera's followers would be possible in a
well-educated nation. It is pitiable
to find it proposed to establish **Technical Education.**
an independent republic,—a hostile
state,—on England's western border. Surely it
ought to be manifest that the devastation of

23

Introduction

Ireland would be an inevitable preliminary, even though, as some Republicans prophesy, an American fleet were riding in Blacksod Bay in western Mayo, one of the finest harbours in the world. Nothing but education can eradicate such mad, unprofitable dreams. Bad as education in the broad sense now is in Ireland, the want of facilities for special or technical training is still more noticeable. On the 22nd June of this year, 1929, the *New Statesman*, a journal dedicated to culture and the higher study of politics, stated that " the bread and butter value of education is being brought home in a very unpleasant way, by the discovery that in the City of Cork facilities for technical training are so poor that Ford's factory, which next to the Shannon scheme, is our industrial hope, has been compelled to recruit its apprentices from England. Unfortunately this is not an isolated instance. When the Carlow sugar-beet factory was opened it was found impossible to unearth in the whole of the Free State a couple of electricians capable of taking charge of the main switchboard ; and, in spite of the millions spent on the Shannon, little or nothing has been done to ensure that when the current is available an adequate number of Irish workers will be forthcoming to wire up the houses."

This is a pitiable state of things, due entirely to the utter neglect of education for centuries by every British government and at the present day to the poverty of the Free State. There is little hope unless Irish American munificence comes to our help.

Introduction

I must add that the more wealthy men of Irish origin keep clear of politics in Ireland the better. In the past their money has often fallen into unworthy hands. What Ireland needs is intellectual " uplift," to use a word dear to Americans. It is little use being " a nation once again " unless the inherent, hereditary culture of our ancient race is reborn and developed. The Jews of New York have set an admirable example in subscribing £5,000,000 for the development of their home land in Palestine. Irishmen in the United States should set their faces like granite against all talk about war. War is hell and war is idiotic. Ireland can gain all she needs by the intelligent use of the vote. Lying side by side with England we must try to live in peace, but there is much that needs reform. Goodwill should take the place of bigotry and misunderstanding.

Contents

Contents

27

Contents

CHAPTER III

CHAPTER IV

CHAPTER V

CHAPTER VI

CHAPTER VII

Contents

CHAPTER VIII

CHAPTER IX

CHAPTER X

Contents

30

Contents

List of Illustrations

CHAPTER I

ANGLO-AMERICAN RELATIONS

THE ANGLO-SAXON AND THE QUOTA

(i) "Almost as soon as I arrived in England I felt an antagonism to the United States. . . . The relations of the two countries are beginning to assume the same character as that of England and Germany before the War. By her industry and organisation Germany was forging ahead as the first Power in the world, but she lost everything by her arrogance and lack of statesmanship. Will it be Great Britain or the United States who will commit this colossal blunder? If we are far-sighted we will conduct ourselves so as to merit the friendship of all nations, for it is to me conceivable that there may come a time when we will need it."—

> Colonel House—*Letter*
> *to President Wilson,*
> *dated* 30*th July,* 1919

(ii) " Such information as reaches me pictures the President as aware and anxious in respect of the Anglo-American naval dispute. Every returning traveller from England brings new and impressive reports of British dislike and bitterness directed against the United States. There is also the equally unanimous report of a profound suspicion of the purposes of the United States. Friends of Mr. Hoover have told me that he interprets the Geneva

and post-Geneva state of mind, at least in certain quarters
in Britain, as the consequence of an attempt to invest
American purposes with the character and colour of
political imperialism.''—

Mr. Frank H. Simonds
in the *Sunday Times* of
the 24th March, 1929.

It is remarkable to find two very distinguished
Americans adopting, with an interval of ten years,
very similar words of warning and
Racial Antagonism. anxiety. Mr. Hoover, like his
predecessor, Mr. Coolidge, is dis-
turbed by the uncertainties of racial antagonism.
All four men are, no doubt, whole-heartedly lovers
of peace, but it is very doubtful whether any of
them or all of them can influence very much
national opinion towards peace. Such is the inherent combativeness of human nature that an
able and, especially, an eloquent statesman can
lead the mob to the shambles, whilst the peace-
maker is looked on as a bit of a traitor and a
person to be blackballed in all decent patriotic
society. In this connection it is not easy to
confute the freethinker, who asks what have the
Christian Churches been doing to restrain the
blood guilt of the nations. In many cases the
ministers of religion have been the loudest and
bitterest in their incitements to war and national
hatreds. It is inspiring to see at Geneva laymen
of goodwill striving to advance the cause of peace,

the socialist often being the most insistent. During
the late war only His Holiness the Pope proclaimed the divine necessity of loving, not killing,
those of a different race or creed.

It is said that the United States will some day
grasp the trident and dominate the
Seven Seas. A little thought will   All the
Trumps.
show that that day is far distant,
because the British Empire holds practically all
the trumps in the naval game. There exists a
combination which, though now entirely pacific,
can make this dream more hopeless than were
the yearnings of Germany in the same direction
before the war. Sea supremacy is the offspring
very much more of naval bases than of naval
strength in battleships and cruisers. Petrol and
the submarine have utterly changed the outlook
of patriotic and ambitious admirals. Modern
battleships are more expensive to maintain than
to build, and need repairing-docks every few
thousand miles. The supply of fuel is an even
more instant difficulty. The arrival of petrol has
made undersea warfare a surpassing terror, and
shoals of submarines can roam the ocean, if they
have refuelling bases, such as England, and only
England, possesses, in sufficient number. Her
allies, France and Japan,—if not quite her allies,
yet her well-wishers in any dispute with the United
States,—would supplement her naval bases by
dozens of well-munitioned harbours. For the purposes of naval war at the present time the United
States seem safely imprisoned in the Western

The Irish Future

Hemisphere. It is very doubtful that the Great Republic will accept this position meekly, but it is quite manifest to the trained naval mind that even if she were to double or quadruple her fleet she would still be practically innocuous to Great Britain. Warships could not get across and stay across the ocean, except, as in 1917, by British help.

As this book goes to press the Prime Minister of England, Mr. J. Ramsay Macdonald, has started for Washington on a mission of peace and good will and amid the blessings of all right-minded men. He seeks to smooth over the difficult and dangerous implications of naval rivalry. In the present state of public feeling in the United States, I fear that little progress can be made. Even though a few cruisers may be scrapped, that is only a drop in the ocean. What is needed is an intelligent and, above all things, an honest and sincere attempt to build up real kindliness between the nations themselves and between the nationalities that make up these nations. There are deadly feuds in the air that need composing first.

The world politics of the next half century will be,—indeed since the war they must be,—a struggle **The Commercial Armageddon.** between England and the United States for the trade of the world. Its circumstances cannot tend towards much good will. Commercial rivalry never has smoothened the path of international relations, but it would be particularly unfortunate if this antagonism were further embittered by racial feeling. It is the biggest mistake conceivable to imagine that in the future the United States will or can be in themselves self-contained or self-sufficing. Like the Germany that has passed away, they must seek a place in the sun, in the sun of Africa and in the sun of Asia. Many and great are the raw materials North America produces, but her demands are spreading all over the earth. An even more urgent need, however, will force her into foreign commercial adventure. She is producing very much more in the way of manu-factured articles than she can possibly consume within her own limits. She must, therefore, find markets for her enormous and increasing industrial output, from motor-cars to coal. To pay for her raw materials from Asia and Africa she must sell largely in both these continents, but her chief markets will probably be found in Europe and for the resultant trade she will desire a foothold in Europe, just as we have been forced to secure innumerable distributing centres all the world over. For the past two or three centuries no nation on earth has had such an able and far-sighted commercial foreign policy as Great Britain. Truly the sun never sets on its works, and it has built up a marvellous network of traffic in every continent and on every ocean, from Canada to Shanghai and from Gibraltar to Melbourne. Her vast fleet and innumerable coaling stations are masters on every sea and strongholds on every trade route.

We must, in fact, recognize as the main anxiety

of our future national well-being that the United
States are certain to seek by every means in
their power a large slice of world

An Irish Dream. trade and that, with their great
wealth and immensely developed mer-
cantile fleet, they are certain to obtain it. If America
and Great Britain were sincere friends it would
be possible to work out a system of partnership
and division of trade, but if there is little goodwill the methods of peace will be at a discount.
I do not say that Irish influence in America is
anything like dominant, but it is growing in
strength and *is not necessarily anti-English.* Indeed, Irish " agitators," as they are called, when
visiting the States in years gone by, have been
taken aback by the apathy of the more influential
and wealthy Irish Americans. I have heard them
speak of this class with extraordinary virulence
as the meanest and basest of mankind. Indeed,
up to very recent times this powerful body hoped
most keenly for a solution of the old Anglo-Irish
dispute. Mr. Roosevelt remarked that " every
Irish family that acquired wealth and culture
desired nothing so much as to get a foothold in
the upper circles of the American portion of the
community." This feeling is changed utterly and,
though successful Irish Americans,—they include
millionaires by the score,—still refuse to give
much countenance to extremists, they have been
deeply moved by recent events. They don't say
much,—things are not sufficiently ripe,—and certainly write less, but the dream of those of them

who study foreign politics, and they are very many, is to see Ireland an emporium of American trade and possibly an ally of the American Union. I have met a few of this class, who even many years ago foresaw such a possibility. Long before the War, an observant visitor to the United States wrote, as quoted by Mr. Lilly in the *Nineteenth Century*, " Large numbers of American Irishmen of education and distinguished positions are bent on combining the advance of American power with the vindication and restoration of Irish independence." The magnificent harbours of Ireland are a big temptation to a trade-seeking nation. The dream would be a vague folly, a *chimæra bombinans in vacuo*, if the Irish people did not stand on the eastern shore of the Atlantic holding out its hands and begging for, at least, economic help from a sympathetic people, and a people probably not unwilling to secure an important trade advantage in Europe. Of a truth the Irish question is not only an English question and an American question, but in very fact a World Question.

It seems a very important question to ask whether it is not possible so to influence Irish feeling that it might become the cement between the English-speaking **Anglo-Saxon Domineering.** peoples instead of being, as it now is, the wedge of disunion. *This is not a Quixotic hope.* It is, in fact, a very possible one, but the " Anglo-Saxon " must give up his domineering. In the United States he is a Junker, fortunately not of the Prussian type, for he is a most easy-going man, essentially *bonhomme*, but in his eyes no other race or class counts for much in politics or social matters. If he does not mind his ways it is certain that the non-Anglo-Saxon elements will unite under Irish leadership and found a third party kindly to the Jew, kindly to the Catholic, kindly to the Negro, and especially kindly to the German, the Italian, the Pole, and other European races. Long before the middle of this century a Labour Party, as in England, will come to the top, made up for the most part of these nationalities and filled by anti-English bias.

Nothing can be more regrettable than the very mention of these religious and racial segregations, but it is the Anglo-Saxon who has started them, and it is the Anglo-Saxon who must make a beginning of goodwill.

The development of the Ku Klux Klan is in itself not very important, but it is symptomatic. It expresses in a fashion, half farcical **The Ku Klux Klan.** and half brutal, what is at the bottom of the minds of a very large section of the old English and Protestant inhabitants of many States. But for its excesses, it would be easy to sympathise with an older aristocracy pushed from its stools by a flood of aliens and heretics, but the white-robed knights are very bad politicians. They are welding into a firm mass men of many races, who seek nothing but equality, equality of treatment and equality of opportunity. This semi-racial feud is being

further embittered by the attempt, insane in a
Republic, dominated by manhood and womanhood
suffrage, to destroy Trades Unions, Railway Brother-
hoods, and the many other confederacies of Labour.

The religious side to the Ku Klux Klan movement is even more lamentable. Above all things
it is anti-Catholic, as are the ubiqui-   The Anti-
tous Shriners, every man a Free-   Catholic
mason, in whose fantastic uniform   Movement.
the late President, Mr. Harding, was so unwise
as to bedeck himself. The chief object of these
societies is above all things to exclude Catholics
from high office. As long as this policy was
kept inside the lodges of Freemasonry, where it
has been both active and effective for many a
year, it was not so noticeable, but it is daily becoming more necessary for the largest religious
community in the States to take measures for
its own protection. Up to now this wicked movement has done little positive wrong in the States,
but in Canada, where Catholics are a minority,
Ku Klux Orangeism has in a very few years given
fifty-three Catholic institutions to the flames, the
two principal Cathedrals of Quebec, convents,
schools, homes for the blind, the incurable, and
the dying. At the same time it is noticeable
that ostracism on the ground of religion does not
exist in Canada in regard to the highest offices
of State. To my mind nothing is more certain
than that, with fair treatment in Washington,
Toronto, and Belfast, American Catholics would
become the most earnest and convinced workers

for goodwill, if not for actual alliance, between Great Britain and the United States. They are already glad to let bygones be bygones, but the present " Anglo-Saxon " atmosphere in North America is a constant reminder of what very unpleasant realities these bygones were. Writing on the subject of " Religion and Politics " in the United States, Sir A. Maurice Low, the Washington Correspondent of the very anti-Irish *Morning Post*, in its issue of the 5th February, 1924, remarks : " There is no State Church in the United States, and there is no constitutional religious disability. Mr. Alfred E. Smith is the Governor of New York. He is an Irishman, a Roman Catholic, and self-made. Even his political opponents admit his ability and his high personal integrity. What more natural than that he should be considered in connection with the Democratic nomination for the Presidency. Governor Smith is barred by his religion. The narrowness of Puritanism, prejudice, bigotry, fear, and intolerance will not permit it." The language used to this gentleman and his religion was fœtid in its grossness. It was by this means that the Negro in the Southern States was got at. There was no objection to his exercising the franchise provided it was used against the Irish Catholic. It was by these unclean methods that four States of the solid Democratic South were converted from their old political creed.

Mr. Lester Walton, a leading Negro publicist has recently been discussing in the *Outlook* of

The Irish Future

New York, the political prospects of his people, who are beginning to perceive that the Ku Klux Klan is equally hostile to the Catholic and to the coloured populations. **Catholics and the Negro.** He gives many instances of their working together at elections in Kentucky, Delaware, Chicago, Maryland, Florida, and Missouri. " One of the reactions " he says " from Ku Kluxism is the growing increase in the number of Negroes embracing the Catholic faith." The Florida *Sentinel* and the *Star of Zion*, both Negro organs, speak of the kindly and " humanitarian " work of the Knights of Columbus, an Irish society, in the Negro camps in France during the late War. The Catholics authorities all over the States urge the necessity of Christian treatment of the ex-slaves and vigorously condemn lynchings, which are everywhere the work of Protestant mobs.

It is most encouraging to note that the ancient hostility to Irishmen, as Irishmen, has nearly died out. Distinguished men of our blood occupy at the present **The Sectarian Barrier.** day the highest offices, such as Mr. Mellon, the Secretary to the Treasury, and Mr. Kellogg, the Secretary of State, as in the past did Mr. Tom Cannon, Mr. Mark Hanna, Mr. Choate, General Casey, who gave to Washington its most beautiful building, the Library of Congress, and Mr. Corcoran, who endowed the American capital with its Art Gallery, side by side with the White House, built by an Irishman on the model of the Duke of Leinster's home at Carton near

The Irish Future

Dublin. This is all to the good, but these gentlemen had all withdrawn from the older faith. The sectarian barrier must be pulled down or 20,000,000 Catholics will know the reason why. When will a Catholic represent the States at the Court of St. James's as the Catholic, Sir Esmé Howard, represents England at Washington?

It is, no doubt, very difficult to visualise the future of the world, but the little we can foresee is a warning to the United States **The Balance of Power Again.** to go slow. I am inclined to think that they would be wise to encourage a large British fleet, for it may be foretold that their extraordinary commercial activity will arouse envy and, as many think, hostility on the part of some of the Great Powers. There seems to be growing up in the States an arrogance of thought and of manner indicating a new and more widespread contest of ambitions, which cannot make straight the path to international tranquillity. A French senator, the distinguished M. Jouvenel, recently announced his conviction that if war recommenced to-morrow it would find England and the U.S.A. on different sides. The intimate friendship, encouraged by Sir Austin Chamberlain, between England and France is believed by most Americans to be based on a renewal of the policy of the Balance of Power, which drew them together twenty years ago. It is pretty certain that Japan is ready and willing to be a third in such a combination. Spain has no reason to be friendly to the United States, which used her so extremely ill, whilst all the races of Spanish and Portuguese origin in South America regard the Munro Doctrine with bitter hostility and eagerly hope that they may find in Europe some kind friend to draw its teeth. When Russia awakens from its communist nightmare it is safe to say that it will not seek an American alliance. Canada does not love her next-door neighbour, and the Tariff taxes and the Quota policy are killing goodwill in nearly every other nation in the world. It is a matter of intense regret, but I am absolutely convinced that the opinion of many watchful politicians is well-founded, and that there is the possibility of a more universal and powerful alliance against the United States than Germany had to meet in 1914.

The enthusiasm with which M. Briand's proposal to establish an United States of Europe has been received is an index finger pointing to exactly the state of things fore- **Arrogance.** seen by Colonel House in the letter to President Wilson, quoted at the top of this chapter. He undoubtedly was warning his own countrymen against "arrogance and lack of statesmanship." That was ten years ago. He added "If we are farsighted we will conduct ourselves so as to merit the friendship of all nations." The Quota Policy is rank arrogance, and the extreme Tariff taxation a gross lack of statesmanship. On the 1st of this month, October 1929, Lord D'Abernon, speaking at Montevideo voiced general opinion on the latter subject in these words :

The Irish Future

" The main object of our Mission to South America is to gain information regarding commercial and industrial conditions and to devise means for increasing the considerable exchanges of produce which now take place between our two countries. I know that there are in some countries those who believe that these exchanges should be all in one direction, that it is possible for a country to do nothing but export, to shut out all imports and to receive nothing but gold. What precisely you would do with the gold is not explained. The whole conception appears to me fantastic. The result aimed at is not attainable, and, if attained, would be undesirable. International trade is essentially interchange, and if you stop the circuit at one point you diminish the whole flow of commerce."

Again and again I would say the United States had better go slow and warily and not to shut out imports.

Other far-seeing Americans have also recently struck a note of anxiety in strong language. In the *American Review* of July, 1928, Mr. Franklin Roosevelt plainly declared " We are certainly far from popular in Canada ; we are slightly better off than last year in Mexico, but in the sixteen republics of Central and South America the United States Government by its recent policies has allowed a dislike and mistrust of long standing to grow into something like positive hatred and fear." So far for the Western Hemisphere, but his remarks on the Great War subsidies are equally

46

significant. " Our Government," he wrote " loaned to Europe during the war about 10,000 millions of dollars. It will receive in return (over a period of years, to be sure), about 22,000 millions. In a time of general poverty and retrenchment our Government has seemed greedy."

The number of Americans of British origin is capable of some statistical examination. It has been ridiculously exaggerated. The **British Immigrants very few from 1775 to 1875.** first Census of the United States was held in 1790 and showed a total population of almost exactly 4,000,000, including about three quarters of a million of negroes and Indians. The white population was thus the not very imposing total of three and a quarter millions. The Dutch, Irish, and Germans, had already come in in very great numbers, as shown by the military returns of Washington's army. Mr. Roosevelt in his *New York* shows that they were more than half of the population of that city. Even the earliest settlers were not exclusively English. There is evidence of settlements of French mostly in the Mississippi Valley and Louisiana. A party of five hundred from Normandy are mentioned in the records of Ohio as having perished in its forests. Florida was Spanish and Swedes colonized the shores of the Delaware. Indeed, the vast growth of later years did not begin for half a century later, the white population having increased in 1830 only to ten and a half millions, an expansion due almost entirely to natural causes, a prolific birth-rate, generally well over thirty per thousand, during forty years. Immigration began to tell in the following decades, the white population being doubled in twenty years. By 1860 the total population had increased, mostly by a great influx of Irish and Germans, to 31,500,000, of whom, however, 4,000,000 were negroes. Arrivals from Europe rapidly increased the growth of the nation in the next four decades, the white population advancing in 1900 to 67,000,000, whilst the black numbered 9,000,000 more.

I have been at much trouble to discover but have been unable to trace many incomers from England during the latter part of **Irish from England.** the nineteenth century, that is in the crucial period 1860 to 1910. Great Britain was at that period the most prosperous and wealthy country in the world and itself attracted immigrants, mostly from Ireland. In every large manufacturing town in England great colonies of Irish grew up, some two millions in all, it was estimated. They were in most part assimilated in that country, and an appreciable number of them became British Labour leaders, four of them rising to cabinet rank in the first Labour Government of 1924. A large section, however, did not fall into line with their English neighbours and remained Catholic, Nationalist and restless. In a few years, when they had saved enough money, they fled across the Atlantic and, with their English training in factories and industrial occupations, became excellent American citizens. Tammany received them with open arms and placed them in lucrative employments. It is certain that in the statistics of immigration these men and their families were returned as of English origin. They were, as a matter of fact, very anti-English.

The *Statesman's Year Book* gives a very valuable table of the principal foreign-born populations of the United States in 1900. Their total was 10,356,644. It comes from official American sources and is reproduced below.

English Immigrants only 8 per cent.

England	..	..	..	842,078
Wales ..	..	..	..	93,682
Scotland	..	..	..	233,977
Ireland	..	..	..	1,618,567
Total United Kingdom		..	..	2,788,304
Germany	..	..	..	2,666,990
Canada and Newfoundland	..	..	1,181,255
Sweden ..	..	..	..	573,040
Norway	..	..	..	336,985
Russia ..	..	..	..	424,096
Italy ..	..	..	..	484,207
Poland ..	..	..	..	383,510
Denmark	..	..	..	154,284
Austria ..	..	..	..	276,249
Bohemia	..	..	..	156,991
France ..	..	..	..	104,341
Hungary	..	..	..	145,802

The Irish Future

The outstanding fact is that the immigrants of English origin were only one-twelfth part of the foreign-born population, that is, roundly, only eight in every hundred, whilst Germany sent 26 per cent. and Ireland 16. The immigrants from the three Celtic nationalities, Ireland, Scotland, and Wales, numbered 1,996,000, or, roundly, 20 per cent., much more than double of the English contingent, which was smaller than that from Sweden and Norway combined and from Italy and Poland combined. The immense influx of Germans gives an idea of the power that this highly educated and hard-working people wield and in the future will yield in ever-increasing vigour.

Indeed, after the foundation of the American Union, immigration from England in any appreciable quantity seemed to stop and did not begin again for a hundred years. The emigrating Englishman went to Canada and Australia. He avoided the States, where things were made none too pleasant for him. Mr. Roosevelt describes the racial riots in New York and other great cities " during the period covered by the forty years preceding the Civil War," adding that the mobs were " very patriotic and boisterously anti-British." Naturally the English in England replied with considerable vigour, and, naturally too, the Englishman, who desired to emigrate, went anywhere rather than to the United States of America.

With the unwisdom that seems to dog " Anglo-

The Irish Future

Saxon " propaganda one of the first acts of the
new President, Mr. Hoover, in March, 1929, was to
issue a proclamation, which, under
the pretext of " national emigration Political
Gerrymandering.
origins," has utterly upset the old
law of the United States. Its whole object is to
manipulate things in the interests of Great Britain
and the Protestant part of Ireland by an excessive
favour and to injure practically every other
nationality, including the great German, Latin,
and Slavic contingents. The most noteworthy
effect of this policy is to make the very name of
England an object of marked ill-will. The following
are the more objectionable figures, giving the limit
of immigrants admissible in two very recent years.

	1924	1929
Great Britain and Northern Ireland	34,007	65,721
Germany	51,227	25,957
Irish Free State	28,567	17,823
Sweden	9,561	3,314

Following so soon after the candidature of
the Irish Catholic, Mr. A. L. Smith, for the Presidency, the policy of the Quota cannot evade
the suggestion of political gerrymandering. If
this demonstration of racial discrimination and
hostility does not drive the Germans and Catholic
Irish into an alliance, which must disturb American
domestic policy in an anti-English direction, it
will be a wonder. They might begin operations

51

by impressing the fact that the Anglo-Saxons are far from the predominant race, and, in reality, are a diminishing factor in the population in

Birth Control. consequence of their restricted birth-rate and unlimited divorces. The girls from Ireland want no change of husband and, proud of their first baby, are still prouder of their fifth. Their Catholic sisters of Italian and Polish origin, millions of them, are also nation builders, whilst German women are not far behind. Only the so-called Anglo-Saxons are bent on race suicide and ask England to make up the deficit. Can they wonder if Europe does not admire them and their childless wealth?

One of the most shameless defences of the Quota policy appeared a couple of years ago in the *Sunday Times* of London, from the pen of the

Seven out of Forty-Seven. Very Reverend W. Inge, Dean of St. Paul's, in this passage :

" The American-born are barely keeping up their numbers. Every year America becomes less Anglo-Saxon, and recently the largest accessions have come from South Italy and the Slav countries. Employers have encouraged this low-grade immigration because they cannot get Americans to do farm-work and other rough jobs. In many parts the less fertile farms are already derelict, and the fruit rots on the trees. But the danger of saturating the country with inferior stocks has induced the Government to pass the well-known Quota regulations. It was high time, if the Anglo-Saxons are not to be reduced to a small and sterile aristocracy. In New Haven I found 60,000 Italians out of 150,000, and in the beautiful little colonial town of Wallingford the Episcopalian clergyman told me that out of forty-seven births last year, only seven were children of English-speaking parents. And this was in Connecticut, once a purely British settlement. I was delighted to hear that under the revised regulations, which will shortly be enforced, the English contingent is to be largely augmented, the Italian reduced, and the Southern Irish, who are spoken of as an unmitigated nuisance, are to be cut down to a very small number. The Americans are wise; but when shall we, in this overcrowded country, have the sense to pass an Irish Exclusion Act? Lancashire and Western Scotland are already flooded with these undesirables, who will come in even greater numbers when they are forbidden to go to America."

It is only fair to Dean Inge to recognize that, whilst he regrets that New York City has been dominated by Tammany and the Irish for twenty years, that " great **The Most Magnificent City.** untidy and haphazard city is now beyond question the most magnificent of all great cities." That Irish genius, Mr. A. L. Smith, has been the chief power in this wonderful work of progress.

In its issue of the 27th January, 1924, the *Observer*, the influential organ edited by Mr. J. L. Garvin, the most forceful penman on the London Press, did good **Hocus-pocus in Religions.** service by drawing attention to the Immigration Law just introduced in Congress.

He makes it clear that this legislation is intended to hocus-pocus a very difficult question to the disadvantage of Catholic nationalities, although there are no races, to which American development owes more during the past fifty years. It is their brawny arms that have spread out a vast network of railways over the Central and Western States and make American mining industries the success that they are. The *Observer* remarks that " the older Catholic immigration from Ireland and Germany, which has long been here, had practically been absorbed. The country was used to them ; and it would have been difficult to start any movement based on apprehension about their presence if it had not been for the recent increase in the Catholic population " coming from Italy and Poland. This scheme is a manifest gerrymandering of the electorate on the score of religion, and by it the Republican administration is asking for trouble and will get it to the full.

In face of the very high-browed contempt of modern Anglo-Americans for the other races of the Great Republic, I cannot resist the temptation to quote what a pure blue-blooded Anglo-Saxon very recently said about their ancestors. The Honble. Sir John Fortescue, the Historian of the British Army, wrote in the London *Times* of the 6th November, 1925, this striking appreciation :

Rascality and Brutality.

" The Americans were a very curious stock. Virginia in its early days had been peopled chiefly

by criminals. Carolina in the seventeenth century
was a refuge for the rascality of the earth. New
England had been settled mainly by the sourest
and narrowest of fanatics, who prated about
liberty of conscience and desired liberty to perse-
cute. Altogether, if the first American settlers
were to present themselves at New York now, they
would most of them, perhaps not excluding those
on the Mayflower, be consigned at once to Ellis
Island. Better immigrants followed, notably discontented Irish and discontented Highlanders in
the eighteenth century, with a good infusion of
Germans. The descendants of all these folk made
a difficult population to deal with at the best. As
a body they seem to have borne great resemblance
to the Boers of 1899. There was a certain leaven
of highly educated and cultured men and a great
lump of the ignorant and narrow-minded, with a
strong touch of primitive brutality."

This brutality was shown by their horrible
cruelty to the loyal English settlers during the War
of Independence, about 1775.

CHAPTER II

THE IRISH PARTY AND THE PEACE TREATY

THE REAL PARNELL

THE ENGLISH CATHOLICS

"It is to the honour of the Free State Government that it has stretched out the hand of friendship to those of the Anglo-Irish gentry, who have remained on in their ancestral homes, and has sought to utilise their gifts and experiences, in the Senate and elsewhere, in the task of building up again their common patrimony."

> The London *Observer* of
> the 11th August, 1929.

"We have got an admirable Government. I think that no one can fail to admire the ability and skill with which the Government of the Irish Free State have dealt with an extraordinarily difficult situation. They have given us order out of chaos, peace out of war, and security out of very great peril."

"I believe that all through the country there is a growing tendency between Protestants and Catholics, between Unionists and Nationalists, to bury the hatchet and to realise that they were all Irishmen, working for the good of the country."

> The Earl of Wicklow, speaking in
> Trinity College, Dublin, the great
> Protestant University, in June, 1926.

Frank Hugh O'Donnell, of Carndonagh, County Donegal,
M.P. Dungarvan.

The Irish Future

THE Orange Government of Belfast has done much to set Catholics and Protestants at one anothers' throats.

No more improbable state of things can be imagined than that in which the Anglo-Irish Treaty of November, 1921, took its birth. For over half a century a large and vigorous Nationalist party in the House of Commons demanded Self-Government, and it was supported during most of that period by the most powerful Liberal governments of modern times. The extraordinary fact is that this great Home Rule Party had practically nothing to do with the Treaty, which gave Ireland the wide independence of Dominion Status. It had been, in fact, repudiated by the Irish people years before.

A Repudiated Party.

To understand the position it is necessary to go back a long way. The first nation-wide demand for self-government began in 1782, when the Protestants of Ireland, mostly of English origin, took up arms to overthrow the evil and corrupt supremacy of London in Irish affairs. They were successful, and the Act of the British Parliament, known as " 23rd of George III, chapter 28," became law. Its preamble was in these words :

A Corrupt Supremacy.

" Be it enacted that the right claimed by the people of Ireland to be bound only by laws enacted by His Majesty and the Parliament of that Kingdom in all cases whatsoever, shall be, and is hereby declared and ascertained *for ever*, and

shall at no time hereafter be questioned or
questionable."

This, the most perfect solution of the Irish
question, was scrapped eighteen years later by
the Act of Union, by a law denounced by Mr.
Gladstone, who said he knew "no blacker or
fouler transaction in the history of man." A
century earlier the great Fox charac-
Perfect Solution. terised it as "atrocious in its
principles and abominable in its
means," "a measure the most disgraceful ever
carried or proposed." "The sacrifice of
Nationality," wrote Lecky, "was extorted by the
most enormous corruption in the history of representative institutions. It was demanded by no
considerable portion of the Irish people, it was
effected *without a dissolution*, in opposition to
the overwhelming majority of the representatives
of the counties and considerable towns, and to
innumerable addresses from all parts of the country.
The Union was a crime of deepest turpitude, which
by imposing with every circumstance of infamy
a new form of government on a reluctant and
protesting nation has vitiated the whole course
of Irish opinion." The Act of Union was carried
in the Irish Parliament of 300 members by a
majority of 162, of whom 116 were place men in
the pay of the English Government.

The Union was never accepted in Ireland.
Our grandfathers witnessed, in the great Repeal
Agitation of Daniel O'Connell, the first deter-
mined attempt to remove an intolerable wrong.

The Irish Future

I may remark that this was the only purely Irish attempt to reform, and I believe it is the only one that will bring permanent peace. Our fathers' day, in 1874, saw the second attempt, that of the wise Ulster Protestant, Isaac Butt, which for a few years united a considerable body of Conservative Anglo-Irishmen with the old Irish under the banner of Home Rule. They included Lord Francis Conyngham and Sir Colman O'Loghlen, members for County Clare, Lord Robert Montague for Westmeath, Sir George Bowyer for Wexford, Colonel Colthurst for Cork, Mr. O'Connor Don and the Honble. Charles French for Roscommon, Captain King Harman for Sligo, Mr. Errington for Longford, and many other important landlords. This scheme of self-government might have succeeded had English statesmen been more foreseeing and more generous. Both Conservatives and Liberals, however, united in downing it with equal unwisdom, the former looking to coercion as the panacea and the latter basing its hopes on domestic and economic reforms, such as Disestablishment, land legislation and educational facilities, all admirable in themselves, but from the National standpoint almost futile. England ought to know from her wide experience, from Belgium to Italy and from Poland to Egypt, that National feeling once aroused is rarely affected by remedial legislation. It demands a stronger regimen to assuage its imperious and tenacious demands.

It would be a long story to tell how the Home

Rule of Isaac Butt sickened in the hands of the
incompetent Parnell and the Socialist Davitt,
Subservience. and how it died in those of kindly
John Redmond. Under the former
it was practically displaced by the
Land League and its anarchist war on wealthy
Irishmen. Under the latter Home Rule was an
inert survival and little but a name. For four
years in the House of Commons, 1906-10, I watched,
as a London member, its quiet disintegration and
its impotent old age before its death in the short
Easter Rebellion of 1916. I do not think that
the Irish members knew of the anger with which
they were regarded by Nationalist Ireland, whilst
a good-humoured disregard of them and of all
their wishes was their lot in Parliament. Except
for occasional outbursts from John Dillon and
Joe Devlin, no National movement in any assembly
was ever supported by such meek and mild representatives. They had their field days and much
eloquence was wasted on empty benches, but the
Liberal Whip could usually rely on Irish subservience
on other occasions. It was impossible not to feel
that the vivid flame of Irish Nationalism, though
temporarily obscured, would some day burst forth
again and reduce the Do-Nothing Party to ashes.

The Irish Party may, indeed, be said to have
ceased to be a political force in 1905 with the
**A Shameful
Pledge.** advent of the Liberal Party to office
under the Premiership of Sir Henry
Campbell-Bannerman, who had given
a shameful pledge to the Liberal Imperialists,

under Mr. Asquith, to drop the Home Rule policy, immediately after having secured the large Irish vote throughout England and Scotland by the warmest advocacy of the Irish cause. Yea, politics are an unclean thing. In 1910, Home Rule again came to the front and just before the War was accepted by both Houses of Parliament. In Chapter IV, " The Irish in the Great War and How Ireland was driven into Rebellion," I discuss the position in those days of patriotism, passion and calamity.

Even enemies honour the memories of Collins and Griffith as brave and honest men, but they had little training in the diplomatic art needed for drawing up a difficult treaty, especially when pitted against **A One-Sided Treaty.** such experienced men of affairs as Mr. Lloyd George, Mr. Winston Churchill, and Lord Birkenhead. It is impossible to discuss here the many shortcomings of the Treaty, executive and financial. Personally my chief regret is that Ireland has lost the position in the Empire and in the world that once was hers. The British House of Commons was the most effective rostrum in the world. From that mighty pulpit it was possible to send forth appeals for justice or tidings of great joy or sorrow to the nations of the world. Ireland must now be dumb. It is something of a pleasure to an Irishman to feel that the British Parliament is hardly more vocal or interesting. Its members, except those on the Treasury Bench, have been consigned to a position of impotence and dullness.

England may fairly boast that throughout the
nineteenth century a powerful party in the House

Irish Advocacy of Reform. of Commons was the friend and advo-
cate of Liberal ideals in practically
all parts of both hemispheres. The
Italian and the Brazilian, the Slav and the Greek,
acclaimed a great influence for good in successive
British Ministries. I am afraid that this widespread gratitude never recognized that it was to
the Southern Catholic Irish that a very large
share of this good work was due. I need hardly
say that throughout this long period the Northern
or Orange Irish were the persistent enemies of
reform and the persistent friends of reaction, not
only in Ireland but in England and the world over.
Since the time of the first Reform Bill, Members
of Parliament from Southern Ireland formed a
dominating factor in the House of Commons,
whenever a Liberal government was in office.
They made reform possible and received little
thanks, except from the English working-classes,
who from that time have been the faithful friends
of Ireland. Since 1833 it was in the power of
these Irish members to overthrow and oust every
reforming Government and, excepting the Parliament of 1880, this state of things continued till
the end of the nineteenth century. At the General
Election of 1834, which raised Lord Melbourne to
the Premiership, 380 Liberals had seats in the House
and 273 Conservatives. The majority of 107
included 66 Irish members, who could at any
moment have terminated the existence of the

The Irish Future

Government; in fact, the Melbourne Ministry was kept in office by Irish support.

The Times, in those days a very unwise organ of opinion, burst into very violent language and assured its readers that "the Whigs durst not refuse this unprincipled **"An Unprincipled Ruffian."** ruffian [O'Connell], whatever office he chose to lay his hand on." The great Catholic Liberator, however, sought not office for himself but the well-being of his Church, his country, and his people. From 1855 to 1880, the great period of Liberal Legislation, the ministries of Lord John Russell, Lord Palmerston, and Mr. Gladstone were kept in power by Irish support. In 1859 the Liberal majority was 43 and the Irish members numbered 50. In 1865 the Liberal majority of 67 was safeguarded by 56 Irish votes. In the Parliament of 1880 the Liberals were for the first time seemingly independent, but were thrown out of office by 39 Irish members voting against them on the budget of 1883. In 1884 household suffrage in Ireland returned 86 Nationalist members and enabled Gladstone to introduce the first Home Rule Bill. I hope Ireland will never forget the magnificent perseverance of the great statesman in his wise Irish policy, in spite of what Mr. Harold Cox, in the *Edinburgh Review* of January 1928, calls "the extraordinary fury" of Queen Victoria and the Conservatives against his reforms in Ireland. The Royal Family, the beloved bond of Empire in every other part of our vast dominions, has fallen sadly short of great possibilities in the first and greatest of British conquests beyond the seas.

Unfortunately, Mr. Gladstone took action too late. Mr. Parnell had in the years before 1884 emasculated the Irish Party and **Degradation and Parnell.** driven out of it nearly all its members, who were cultured and well born. He replaced them by men of a much lower class, who, though honest, sincere Nationalists, were willing to forward his designs for a small salary. The Right Honble. T. P. O'Connor, M.P., in the second volume of his *Memoirs*, page 62, states that, " As to the rank and file of the Party they were practically paupers." " They were nearly all married men, with small businesses of their own, which had to be managed by their wives." Mr. Parnell retained in his own hand the payment of their mean salaries, which Mr. O'Connor thinks averaged about £240 a year—often less. " It was part of our inner policy to leave both the amounts and the payment of these subsidies entirely in the hands of the treasurer of the Fund," Mr. Parnell or his underling ! " A good part of this money the members had to send home to those poor wives struggling hard to keep a petty business going," often a small public house. Most of them lived in squalor across the river in Lambeth, though there were ample funds to maintain them decently. They were as ignorant and uneducated as they were poor.

Mr. T. P. O'Connor also lets in some light on the life of Mr. Parnell. In the first volume of his

Memoirs, page 339, he relates that "In the early part of 1883 Parnell was in pecuniary difficulties. He had no sure source of income. He gave a dinner to his colleagues at the Café Royal, London. **An Unpaid for Dinner.** The account was, I believe, never paid. As was disclosed years later in the Divorce Court, Parnell had at this time entered into relations with Mrs. O'Shea and was maintaining her household." A good deal of money also went on excursions to Paris. It was in this year the Catholic bishops and people of Ireland raised and paid to this high-spirited gentleman a sum of £38,000 as a testimonial to his worth. Large sums were also about the same time raised in America. Mr. O'Connor, who was one of the money-gleaners, mentions the collection of £8,000 in Philadelphia in a short period. There never was any audit of these large sums. "It was part of our inner policy" to let in as little light as possible.

Mr. T. P. O'Connor was not the chief of Parnell's lieutenants, though perhaps chief of his parliamentary friends and the most useful. Mr. Timothy Healy was politically the foremost of his colleagues. He also has been publishing his memoirs and a sordid book it is, being little more than a *réchauffé* of the mean squabbles within the Home Rule Party during many years. I don't wonder that Parnell called him "a gutter-snipe." He devotes **A Wretched Child.** some of the first pages of his work to an account of Parnell's expulsion from Magdalen

The Irish Future

College, Cambridge, and its cause. *De mortuis nihil nisi bonum* is an admirable principle, but it has its limits. Parnell had seduced a girl " not more than sixteen, of remarkable loveliness " and, when she was about to become a mother, discarded her. The wretched child committed suicide. Parnell's sister, Emily, has told the whole pitiable story in a book, called *A Patriot's Mistake.* Mistake!—and that is how the Irish Party regarded the abomination for some twenty years till another woman, Mrs. O'Shea, and another intrigue came to the surface. There were others. I cannot find one word of reprobation in Mr. Healy's *Memoirs,* and this is the gentleman whom the Conservative Government honored by making him the first Governor-General of the Irish Free State.

I am glad to say that my brother, Mr. Frank Hugh O'Donnell, withdrew from this contaminated party in 1884 and thank God that the present Irish Government, made up mostly of men of humble birth, can hold its head high amongst the rulers of men, as a model of clean living and scrupulous honesty.

Mr. T. P. O'Connor did much to injure the good name of the Irish Party for independence.

He was for many years President **Openly Derided.** of the Home Rule Federation of Great Britain and naturally had the confidence of the Irish voters in English towns. He was always a pushing publicist and about 1890 founded some newspapers as Liberal organs. He was so fortunate as to have the capital very

66

largely subscribed by prominent and wealthy Liberals. I have a list of these gentlemen, with a note of the amounts each found for propaganda in their constituencies. In speaking to me several of them did not conceal what were the motives of their generosity and admitted that they had got good value for their money. The total amount subscribed was, according to the share registers of these companies, the very handsome sum of £46,450. The Irish Party always has had a few self-respecting members of great distinction and, as Lord Balfour wrote, forty years after, of a " wealth of oratory without equal in the whole history of our or perhaps any other Parliament." Alas ! its leaders bartered away its independence and it became the rear-guard of the Liberal forces, being openly derided by the Nationalists of Ireland. It is impossible to forget its feebleness in refusing to help the appeal by a distinguished group of English M.P.'s for justice to India in 1906 in the matter of the Partition of Bengal. Many of the Home Rulers explained to me that it would never do to oppose and annoy Lord Morley, at that time Secretary of State for India. I went vigorously against his mistaken policy and won his esteem.

Having mentioned Mr. T. P. O'Connor none too favourably, it is only right to put on record the signal service he rendered to Great Britain in the Great War. **Risking Mutiny.** It is not too much to say that but for his eloquence and dogged determination to

67

make English policy prevail, the United States would never have entered the alliance against Germany. Down to the third year of the War, in spite of such occurrences as the torpedoing of the *Lusitania*, the Great Republic resolutely held aloof and was forced to do so by the very powerful Irish element in its population and Press. So intensely pro-German were the Irish at the outset of the War that it would be risking something like mutiny in the American army, which has always been more than half Irish, to call on the troops to cross the Atlantic in support of England.

To combat this state of things the British Government, by the advice of the other very anti-German Irishman, Lord Northcliffe, **What One Man Can Do.** wisely sent Mr. O'Connor on a lecturing tour in the States. At first he was received with extreme hostility by Irish audiences and more than once risked personal violence, but he held to his guns and for over a year spoke and spoke again in every city and every hall from New York to San Francisco and north and south. He was backed by ample funds and propaganda literature,—mostly lies. The American Irish were in large part won over or shaken, and though they voted a second time for Mr. Woodrow Wilson as President, on his distinct pledge to keep the United States out of the war, they had lost their solidarity and threw over their old friends, the Catholic Germans, a powerful community. The latter had, in due course, their revenge, and voted in a body against Mr. A. L. Smith, the Irish candidate for the Presidency a year ago. Mr. T. P. O'Connor was, it has been stated, offered and declined a peerage, an honour that was more than earned by his great services to England.

One of the strangest and, to Irish Catholics, one of the most painful incidents of our struggle for a better political status within the Empire is the extraordinary ill- **English Catholics.** will we have had to encounter from English Catholics. The Irish immigration into Great Britain has been very large during the past two centuries, but in the eighteenth it was mostly absorbed into the English population and supplied large contingents to Nonconformist congregations and ministries. Famine in Ireland and the immense development of manufactures in England after 1845 drove or attracted myriads of Irishmen to seek food and work in Great Britain. English Catholics were very few, and down to the end of the nineteenth century nine-tenths of the priesthood and more than a half of the bishops bore very pronounced Irish names. The pennies of the poor Irish labourers in English industrial areas built up a thousand churches to the Living God and erected as many schools for an almost slum population. Even in these early days there was little good will in English Catholic circles. An almost incredible fact is that Daniel O'Connell, who won Catholic Emancipation for Englishman and Irishman alike in 1829, when he visited London, was promptly blackballed by the little English Catholic Club or Association of those days. During the recent Centenary Celebrations in London the very name of the Clare election has been overlooked, and it was never mentioned that in order to obtain justice the Duke of Wellington used the threat of insurrection by the five millions of Irish Catholics. The English quarter million was entirely without influence. It is a lamentable fact that the Irish, in their constitutional efforts to obtain religious freedom and self-government, were denied any sympathy by men of their own faith and had to depend for help on Protestants and especially on Nonconformists.

The Anglo-Catholic influence at Rome has been both actively and successfully anti-Irish. It truly claimed that it prevented the learned **An Italian and a Spaniard.** and Nationalist Dr. Walsh, archbishop of Dublin, from receiving the Cardinal's hat. There are two areas in England, in which a very large Irish population has congregated, Lancashire and South London. In both there are dozens of Irish priests in every way fitted for the holy office of the episcopate, but anti-Irish Cardinals have secured in recent years the appointment of an Italian to the first and of a Spaniard to the second, the Most Reverend Monsignori Casartelli and Amigo, both bishops of great distinction, but they had no sympathy with Irish feeling. When Archbishop Mannix left Melbourne a few years ago his bodyguard consisted of thirteen Irishmen who had won the V.C. in the late War, but he found every Catholic door in London closed in his face. It is, indeed, not too much to say that every Irishman is rigorously ostracised in English Catholic society, though by his public services, his abilities, or his wealth, he is gladly received in Protestant houses of distinction. During the period I was a member of Parliament for London, 1906-10, I was invited to the Mansion House, as a matter of course, till a Catholic, Sir John Knill, became Lord Mayor. During his year of office I was not *persona grata*, and every Irish Catholic M.P. has had similar experiences, unless he was a Conservative.

An extremely bad example of the neglect of a manifest duty by English Catholics is connected with the recent troubles in Ireland. The Catholic Union of Great Britain **Due Abhorrence.** rightly condemned in the most vigorous language the outrages committed by Sinn Fein fanatics and criminals, but left to the Archbishop of Canterbury, Lord Robert Cecil, and a hundred other distinguished Protestants the due abhorrence of the Black and Tan terror. English Catholicism was silent when a large Catholic population was driven from their homes in Belfast and contributed not a penny to the fund, raised by Irish and American Catholics, to feed some 10,000 Catholic women and children. The expulsed Catholic men were nearly as numerous and included 3,000 who had fought for England on the fields of France.

I cannot exaggerate the mischief done to

The Irish Future

England and to religion by this infatuated conduct. It embitters racial feeling and has driven thousands of Irishmen into the ranks of Communism and irreligion.

Lost the Faith.

I heard a frantic Irish working man assuring a Labour audience that he would rather wash the feet of a Belfast Orangeman than shake the hand of an English Catholic! There have been during the past half-century very many notable conversions to my religion from the best class of Englishmen, but I mourn that an infinitely larger number of my countrymen have lost the faith and everywhere through England form the most active preachers of anti-British propaganda and Socialist heresies. The short-sighted and unwise action of well-born English Catholics is, no doubt, connected with the fact that for two centuries they were the victims of an oppressive bigotry, which resulted in a narrowness of outlook that unfitted them for the higher duties of political and social life. A similar degeneracy existed, no doubt, in Ireland in the same class. The small Irish Catholic squire, instead of helping to raise his fellow countrymen, has long been their most vicious critic and fawned on London Society.

I repeat at the end of this chapter what I have said at the beginning of this book. The Irish race can render no greater service to mankind than by laying aside old enmities, but it may fairly ask that a policy of good will should also be extended to itself.

Good Will.

His Eminence Patrick O'Donnell, Cardinal Archbishop
of Armagh.

CHAPTER III

ULSTER AND PARTITION

(i) "Glory to God! My eyes shall see the ransomed fields of Down."

Gavan Duffy,
The Muster of the North.

(ii) "Northern Ireland fears a Socialist Government. *Lord Craigavon's Government enjoys important sub-sidies from the British Treasury. The balancing of its Budget depends upon them,* and it lives in the fear that under a Socialist regime in England these sub-sidies might be reduced or might vanish altogether. The Irish Free State's position is more fortunate, for it has ceased to be directly dependent on any Britsh Government."

The Times, of 3rd June, 1929.

THE suggestion that the Partition of Ireland should be recognised as a permanent settlement is wholly inadmissible. Ulster is an integral portion of our motherland and in a very real way a holy land to all Irishmen, who are not West Britons. Irish history is not a strong point in English universities

Our Holy Land.

or schools. Anyhow, it is forgotten that Ulster
was the last home of Irish freedom, and that this
fair province was not conquered till the beginning
of the seventeenth century. Before the reign of
James I it was the patrimony of O'Neil, Earl
of Tyrone, and of O'Donnell, Earl of Tyrconnell,
the former ruling three counties on the east and
the latter three counties on the west. During
the four centuries that followed the first English
invasion in the reign of Henry II, there were
no doubt British raids into Ulster, but they always
were driven back till, in the reign of Elizabeth,
the great and final struggle was decided by England
putting into the field the largest army that had
ever up to then left her shores, much larger than
she employed to conquer France two centuries
before.

The defeat of the Northern Earls was followed
by a merciless confiscation of every acre of their
vast properties and their subjects,
Merciless Confiscation. after a murderous diminution by
massacre, were reduced to the
position of agricultural labourers. The Irish
gentry of Ulster also were forced down to the
same humble position, if they were fortunate
enough to escape with their lives, awaiting an
opportunity to fly to France or Spain where,
as soldiers of fortune, they won military renown
and sometimes founded families of great distinction. Many of the humbler tribesmen, who survived, found a rough existence in the wild
highlands which form so large a part of western

The Irish Future

Ulster, chiefly Donegal, but a large body remained in the plains as the servants of their new masters, mostly Scotch. Many of them gave up their old faith and in time became more anti-Irish than the English themselves, as is the way of renegades. O'Neil and O'Kane are amongst the Orange heirarchy. They frequently changed their names, though they retained for a few generations their Gaelic speech, which was also the tongue of their new Scottish landlords. Both races, however, soon found the necessity of union. Bad land laws formed the bond that brought Protestant and Catholic together. Excessive rents and evictions, in order to supplant men by cattle, drove the peasantry to violence and in a few years the attractions of American freedom and rentless farms induced 200,000 Ulster people to cross the Atlantic. They were mostly of purely Irish origin, working under Scotch guidance. One of the results of this emigration was that the Catholics from the mountains came down to the plains to occupy the abandoned farms of the fleeing Scotch. They were willing to pay or to try to pay the excessive rentals.

It would be a long story to recount Ulster history from those days to the present, but it suffices to say that as the years passed the Northern Province be- *Cultured English Gentlemen.* came a hot-bed of religious strife, which was fostered by the British Government as an inexpensive method of restraining Nationalist agitation. Even in the end of the nineteenth

75

century the Catholics remained in a practically helot condition, except in the western counties. A short time before the Great War the following almost incredible position existed in Belfast, where Catholics formed one-third of the population. There were 437 salaried officials in the service of the Belfast Corporation. Of these, nine were Catholics, probably scavengers, as their total salaries amounted to £765, or about thirty shillings a week. The Protestant employees secured £67,958 every year. The Harbour Board which spent £11,000 on salaries, had not a single Catholic employee, whilst the Poor Law Board, spending £10,000 a year, paid £45 to one Catholic! And Lord Carson told us that the Protestants must fight to save themselves from oppression! Even cultured English gentlemen were not ashamed quite recently to approve of this state of things and to malign the sufferers. Lord Hugh Cecil, M.P., denouncing Home Rule in 1912 in a speech at Belfast, anticipated that the Irish nation, " this precious nation that is to be erected, will be the most squalid and sordid thing that the world has ever seen." The treatment of Irish Catholics in Belfast is intended to produce such a population. It is facts and insults like these that drive Irishmen to the verge and past the verge of passionate despair. It is little wonder that a most distinguished English Conservative M.P., Sir Mark Sykes, a few years ago denounced in *The Times* the picture of Irish Catholics as " an idolatrous and brutish horde." It is almost

The Irish Future

incredible that a great Briton, Thomas Carlyle, could write the following sentences, " The Celt of Connemara is a savage and a liar and if no beneficent hand will chain him into wholesome slavery, and with whip on back or otherwise, try to tame him and get some work out of him, nature **" Exterminate like Wolves."** herself, intent to have her world tilled, has no resource but to exterminate him, as she has done the wolves." There should be an expurgated edition of the writings of this Scotch Nietzsche. The condition of Ulster Catholics after the Dublin rebellion of 1916 was a nightmare which may be summarized in the one fact that some 10,000 Catholic men, mostly employed in the ship-building yards and including nearly 3,000 ex-soldiers, were driven from their homes in Belfast, burnt out for the most part. It was a bloody time, nearly 500, mostly Catholics, being killed.

In 1922 the separate Ulster Government was set up and, had it acted with impartiality, bygones might be bygones. The Free State Government in its treatment of **Ostracism of Catholics.** Protestants set an admirable example by, in the first place, apportioning half the seats in the Senate to Protestants. Not a single Catholic found his way into the Belfast Upper Chamber. There is not the least evidence or the smallest suggestion that during the past seven years any law has been passed by the Dail Eireann or any administrative action taken by any of its departments, which injures in the least any Protestant individual or any Protestant interest. The exact contrary is the fact in the six Northern Counties. The Catholics have been *disfranchised*, as far as the Belfast Parliament can effect this end, both in regard to elections for the Imperial Parliament and for municipal councils. In no part of these six counties can the Catholics now make their views prevail in regard to police, education, sanitation, poor law, religious facilities and the hundred other things that affect everyday life. They have been driven out of every position of influence they held in 1922, and this oppression has been effected by hostile *legislation* in Belfast.

These facts have been concealed from public opinion in England, although they reveal a state of things that makes political **"In Solitary Infamy."** settlement in Ireland wholly hopeless and creates a condition most dangerous to the British Empire—a certain source of trouble, if not of disorder and bloodshed. It reminds me of the language of Lord Acton, the great English historian, in one of his *Essays*, " The system applied to Ireland, which uses religious disabilities for the purpose of political oppression, stands alone in solitary infamy amongst the crimes and follies of the rulers of men." There is no finer man in the British Empire than the Ulster Protestant, but there is no more persistent tyrant than the Orange Lodge. The difficulties in which Mr. Cosgrave's

The Irish Future

Government is involved by " Republican " hostility, is chiefly due to the belief that he has been slack in defending the Catholic subjects of the Northern State.

It is a great pleasure to recognise that British fair play incorporated in the English Act of 1922, which gave constitutions to both the Free State and the six Northern Counties, a wise and just provision securing to minorities in both areas the advantage of Proportionate Representation. The Dublin Government has loyally maintained this equitable arrangement, but one of the first acts of the Belfast Parliament has been to abrogate it, to the great injury of the Ulster Catholics. I believe that this Orange legislation was *ultra vires,* but the late Conservative Government in England has condoned and maintained the wrong. For many years West Belfast was worthily represented by Mr. Joseph Devlin in the Imperial Parliament —a serious offence to Orange intolerance. By the inclusion of two Protestant wards, Shankhill and Woodvale, in this constituency, Catholic representation has been effectively wiped out in Belfast. Although 34 per cent. of the total population of the Six Counties are Catholics, they are represented in the House of Commons at the present hour by only two out of seventeen members. One was kept in prison for many months, without trial or even charge laid.

The gerrymandering of electoral areas has been carried out all over the Six Counties by the Belfast

Government. By segregating and combining districts, by twisting internal boundaries, it has **The Twisting of Boundaries.** made sure that in the County Council of Tyrone the Nationalist pre-war majority of six should be changed into an Orange majority of fifteen. In Fermanagh the reduction is from a majority of three to a minority of sixteen. In 1920, before gerrymandering, in the two counties of Tyrone and Fermanagh, in which there is a Catholic majority of 23,000 in the joint population, the Local Government Act (British Parliament) gave eighty-four seats to the Catholics and sixty-five to the Protestants. So gerrymandering was resorted to, with the exhilarating result that the figures were twisted right round. At the most the Catholics can now secure sixty-three seats to eighty-five for the reformed faiths, in spite of their large majority in voters. *In all unions, six in number*, their representatives are now in a minority, whilst formerly they had majorities in four. In Omagh 463 votes are needed to secure the election of a Catholic, whilst 228 Protestants suffice for a Protestant victory. In Protestant Lurgan there was a Catholic minority of six. Not one can now be elected. Can one wonder that Catholics in Southern Ireland have resolved to strain every nerve in order to rescue as many as possible of their co-religionists from a government that, openly and without subterfuge, loads the dice so as to exclude its Catholic subjects from their legitimate influence in even

municipal administration ? Its action is a near imi-
tation of one of the worst features of the Penal Code.
The Right Hon. T. P. O'Connor, P.C., M.P.,
brought these facts to notice some years ago
in a detailed speech, lasting an
hour, in the House of Commons, £15 millions
in Doles.
but it was not reported in the
London Press, that is, in any of the organs of
the various parties—a mean, low-down conceal-
ment of real grievances. Far from doing anything
to amend this monstrous state of things, the
British Government, during the past seven years,
has, according to *The Times* of the 3rd June,
1929, bolstered it up by grants of many millions to
the Ulster Exchequer, in all about fifteen millions.
The Times admits that " the balancing of the Northern Budget depends upon these important subsidies."

The Catholic Bishops of North Eastern Ulster
also condemned this incredible bigotry in the
following words :—" It is doubtful
whether in modern times any parallel "The Fatuity
of Idiots."
can be found for the way in which
the Catholic minority in the North of Ireland is
being systematically wronged under the laws of
the Northern Parliament. The utter disregard for
the rights of Catholics, this ever-advancing aggression on Catholics is a grave menace to the peace
of the whole community, and in view of what
has already happened, after waiting very long
we consider the time has come for our people to
organise openly on constitutional lines and resolve
to lie down no longer under this degrading

F

thraldom." It is not easy to hope for a better understanding. The words of Sydney Smith still hold true, " The moment the very name of Ireland is mentioned the English seem to bid adieu to common feeling, to common prudence, and to common sense and to act with the barbarity of tyrants and the fatuity of idiots." One would naturally regard such language as stupidly exaggerated till the doings of the Blacks and Tans recur to memory and recall the still more horrible language of Mr. Lecky in his great *History of the Eighteenth Century* : " The suppression of the native race was carried out with a ferocity which was hardly exceeded by any page in the bloodstained annals of the Turks." Another great Protestant Irishman, Henry Grattan, a Conservative M.P., as Mr. Lecky was, and an Imperialist of the school of Pitt, declared that " to find a worse Government than that of the English in Ireland you must go to Hell for your policy and to Bedlam for your methods." You must certainly go to Bedlam if you are seeking arguments to explain or justify Partition and the vaunted midnight Treaty or Settlement of London, November, 1921. Under these circumstances how is the vast Irish population in the United States likely to feel and act ?

I often think that my Orange brethren may plead that they are justified in rejecting a government largely composed of Catholics by the lessons they receive from Englishmen of great distinction. I

" Drunken Bliss."

have already quoted Lord Hugh Cecil's appreciation of the Irish nation as " the most squalid and sordid thing that the world has ever seen." The London *Spectator*, the most intellectual organ of the educated classes in England, wrote on the 10th December, 1921 : " Southern Ireland is probably condemned to be one of the worst governed States in the world,—a land of civil disorder and intimidation, overshadowed by the selfish and suffocating power of a reactionary sacerdotal caste." Another Conservative organ, *The Outlook*, published on the 17th October, 1925, an appeal to English Churchmen, ending with this refined poetry :

> Nor let them barter wife and child,
>> bright hearth and happy home
> For the drunken bliss of the strumpet kiss
>> of the Jezebel of Rome.

These sentiments ought to make the scurrilous opponents of Mr. A. L. Smith, the Catholic candidate for the American Presidency, green with envy.

Mrs. Stopford Green, the widow of the greatest of modern English historians, contributed on the 23rd November, 1912, to the *Nation*, a very outspoken article on the "Get Rid of an Irishman." position in Ulster, when the Home Rule Bill was approaching decision in Parliament. She drew attention to the spirit in which the Conservative Party was facing the position.

The Irish Future

" Lord Hugh Cecil passionately reminded his audience that this nation which was to have a parliament in Dublin was a nationality which ' they despise and hate.' He remained splendidly true to the spirit of his father's (Lord Salisbury's) saying that, ' the instinctive feeling of an Englishman is to wish to get rid of an Irishman.' "

" Burn him out," says Belfast. She reminds us of the very serious threat of Mr. Bonar Law to the Liberal ministers that if they applied Home Rule to Ulster " the populace of London would lynch you on their lamp-posts." My object in quoting these deplorable sentiments is that their spirit is still alive, not only in Belfast and London, but in Washington. Mr. Hoover, a thoroughly high-caste man, in his presidential campaign forgot himself so much as to take advantage of an anti-Catholic propaganda. Under the heading " The Dominant Issue " the London *Observer* of the 14th October, 1928, wrote, " there is no calculating the harm that has been done to Smith by the organised, subsidised, and intensive under-cover drive against him because of his religion. Mr. Hoover made a hurried trip to Tennessee, the heart of the bigoted territory, and an owner of a paper devoted to scurrilous abuse of Catholics, and carrying loathsome cartoons of the Pope, was actually invited to be the candidate's train guest ; and numerous members of the Hoover National Committee are waging his fight solely on religious hatreds. Meanwhile, Dr. Nicholas Murray Butler, the most intellectual of the Republican leaders and President of Columbia University, has made a formal protest against this kind of campaign, and suggests that some Gibbon is writing now on the Decline and Fall of Christianity. The election of Mr. Hoover on this issue would make a mockery of the pretence of religious toleration here and leave scars that would abide for generations." There will be no peace in the world whilst the doctrines of hatred are preached or winked at by men of light and leading.

The Catholics of Ulster have plucked up courage to oppose the policy of degradation that the Orangemen would apply to them, and have at once gained a great **The Penal Laws Again.** victory by the return of two M.P.'s to the Imperial Parliament, one of whom, Mr. Devlin, by his eloquence and sincerity will be a tower of strength to his cause. The sooner Englishmen recognise that the Ulster Question is one of extreme urgency the better. The following passage from one of his recent speeches summarises " a condition of things unparalleled in any civilised community at the present time, a gross oppression, modelled on the excesses of Penal Laws in the seventeenth century." At the inauguration of the Catholic National League in August, 1928, Mr. Devlin said : " After waiting for seven years—years of justice denied, disabilities imposed and religious and political inferiority branded upon our people—we have decided to start this organisation."

The Irish Future

" In the entire Senate of the Northern Parliament there is not a single representative of that numerically powerful minority,

"Pariahs and Outcasts." over a third of the population, to which we belong. In the Judiciary, supposed to be the seat of justice and the fount of equity, there is not a single member of the proscribed and penalised creed. The grand juries are selected by high sheriffs, themselves selected by the Government. Even in places such as Derry City and in the counties of Fermanagh and Tyrone, where we are in a definite majority —the latest census figures emphasise that fact— our people have, by methods of juggling and gerrymandering that are without precedent, been placed in a hopeless minority on all the public boards. The doors are closed, locked, and *barred against our people* in every avenue leading to positions of influence in the civil administration. We are treated as pariahs and outcasts in the community in which we are citizens. Our people are excluded from those spheres in which, when allowed adequate opportunity, they have proved themselves not inferior in intellect or capacity or service to those who have constituted themselves their masters."

The plain English of this indictment is that the Imperial Parliament has made over the Ulster

Baptised on the Hillside. Catholics to the torturers and no man of their blood, who has an ounce of spunk in him, will rest till this monstrous intolerance, out of date and

86

shameful to England, has been strangled and stamped out. I write with vigour, as the son of a gallant British soldier, one of an ancient nobility, who was baptised on the hillside in the glens of Donegal because the Orange oppressors had burned down not only his home but the chapel, in which his father worshipped. That was in the beginning of the last century. Things have not improved much in 125 years. There are tens of thousands of Catholic Ulstermen in the United States and they are the most anti-British element in the population. They fled also to Scotland and, especially in Glasgow, form a most subversive population, sending able Communists to the Westminster Parliament.

CHAPTER IV

THE IRISH IN THE GREAT WAR

AND HOW IRELAND WAS DRIVEN INTO REBELLION

(i) "My lords, it is mainly to the Irish Catholics that we owe all our proud predominance in our military career, and that I personally am indebted for the laurels with which you have been pleased to decorate my brow. We must confess, my lords, that without Catholic blood and Catholic valour no victory could have ever been obtained, and the first military talents might have been exerted in vain."—

> The Duke of Wellington in the House of Lords, pleading for Catholic Emancipation.

(ii) "In the Great War one battalion alone lost one hundred and eighty officers and over four thousand rank and file."

> "The Passing of the Munsters."
> *The Times*, 9th June, 1922.

(iii) "An organised war (on Irishmen) was in steady and pitiless operation for two and a half years before it began, early in 1919, to provoke violent reprisals from amongst this tortured people against the agents of the Executive."—

> Mr. Erskine Childers,

88

The Irish Future

(iv) " Things are being done in Ireland which would disgrace the blackest annals of the lowest despotism in Europe."

Mr. Asquith (Earl of Oxford)
in 1921.

(v) " Now that Ireland has ceased to be a factor of any importance in English affairs."—

The New Statesman,
24th November, 1928.

(vi) " The two supreme services which Ireland rendered Great Britain are her accession to the allied cause on the outbreak of the Great War and her withdrawal from the House of Commons at its close."—

Winston Churchill,
The Aftermath, p. 283.

MR. CHURCHILL's note of deep satisfaction at having got rid of the Irish representatives at Westminster is very illuminating. Coming immediately after Ireland **"God Save England."** had given of her best to the British Empire in the preceding decade, it is horrible to Irishmen, especially to those who, like myself, wish nothing but good to the British connection. In 1914 the whole Irish race, including the millions in Australia and other colonies, by wholesale recruiting to the British army, were in practice and reality praying " God Save England " on every fighting front. It was they who gave to that army its first battle ballad, " Tipperary."

Yet in those days of trouble and anxiety the anti-Irish fanatics of Ulster and London were already questioning Irish motives and preparing the great betrayal.

As a matter of fact, no people in the two hemispheres were more convinced of the justice of the war than the Irish Nationalists. An **"Magnificent."** intense kindliness towards France, in spite of the anti-Catholic vagaries of its governments, has always been a wholehearted tradition of Ireland. Had not Germany supplied Mauser rifles to the Orange Army, and had not the Kaiser hobnobbed with Carson at the Kiel Regatta? So Irish Catholics came trooping to the British colours in tens of thousands. Lord Kitchener plainly called them "magnificent." Mr. Redmond, the most violent of anti-German propagandists, was able truthfully to claim that in proportion to population, Ireland sent more of her sons to the British Army in the first three months than any other people within the Empire. Probably the most authoritative statement was made on the 10th of last November, 1928, by Lord Glenavy at Trinity College, of which he is Vice-Chancellor. He was also President of the Senate in Dublin, and altogether the most distinguished Protestant in the Free State. He said that, "of Ireland's whole population about 1,000,000 were fitted by age and physique for active service, and of these *at least* 400,000, or more than one in every three, were numbered in the fighting forces on land and sea." And English statesmen and publicists express with joy their belief that the Empire is well rid of the brethren of those who died for England.

Even the ever-hostile *Morning Post* of the 26th February, 1915, stated that "from the beginning of the war up to the present month 115,513 Irishmen have joined the **"Every man Rejoined."** various regiments of the Army, this figure not including those who have enlisted in many districts, from which returns have not yet been obtained. The overwhelming mass of Irish recruits in Great Britain have joined English, Scottish, and Welsh regiments. One battalion of the King's Liverpool Regiment (Territorials) is purely Irish, and was among the first to volunteer, for foreign service. Glasgow has a total of 8,470 Irish recruits, and the Tyneside Irish Brigade, raised at Newcastle-on-Tyne, is now 5,400 strong. The number of Irish recruits reported from London is 5,460." General Dalrymple, the Colonel-in-Chief of the Connaught Rangers, was able to state that "in a few days after mobilization every man of its reservists had rejoined." Not one failed to take his place in the regiment, though most of them came from the far west of Ireland. More than half of the splendid corps from Australia were Irish Catholics. They won a dozen V.C.'s amongst them. *Out of the Catholic population of Belfast*, Mr. Joseph Devlin, M.P., was able to raise five full regiments to fight in France. The Belfast Orangemen have since been burning down the homes of these brave and loyal men. There was indeed a radical belief in the righteousness of the War and especially that it was being waged for the freedom of a small and wronged nation, Belgium.

Another great Conservative London journal, *The Evening Standard,* described in glowing periods the wonderful change of feeling in the Irish people :

"The Roll of Honour."

"Her flag is in the thick of the battle, and the names of her sons are inscribed on the Roll of Honour. Figures officially compiled up to February 15, 1915, show that there were 100,000 Irishmen from Ireland with the colours. The Irishmen in Great Britain with the colours then numbered 115,000. The Irishmen across the seas who have joined the colours make up a grand total of at least 250,000 Irishmen in the Army. That is a record which never shall be shamed. Ireland has done her part nobly and generously, and therefore to-day the whole Empire ought to rise to its feet, link hands, and sing, ' God Save Ireland ! ' This is the day to remember the name of Michael O'Leary, the Cork lad who won the V.C. by the most daring and desperate valour. His story might have come straight out of the Iliad."

Colonel Repington, the distinguished military correspondent of *The Times* on the 12th November, 1918, denounced "*the besotted policy*" of the British Government towards Ireland, adding "We prefer to remember her by those 200,000 Irishmen *from*

"Besotted Policy."

The Irish Future

Ireland who have fought so valiantly on countless fields of battle and have displayed once more the priceless valour of their race."

And what was their reward? The blackest ingratitude. It was not an Irishman but the Secretary of State for War, Mr. Lloyd George, who in the House of Commons in 1916 denounced the treatment of the Irish soldiers, who rallied with such enthusiasm to the aid of British policy, as "malignant." One might well be astonished by the daring of the Sinn Fein bands till it is remembered that they were guided, trained, and largely composed of demobilized soldiers, actuated by an intense hatred of the nation that treated them both badly and ungratefully. It is impossible to state with fullness the "malignities" that aroused the late Prime Minister's wrath, but the Conservative *Evening Standard*, October, 1916, summarised them in these words : " Ireland was refused a separate badge ; Mr. Asquith's pledge of an Irish Army Corps was not kept ; the Roman Catholic University was not allowed an officers' training corps ; *all commissions were reserved for Protestants*, even in units strictly Catholic ; mention of the gallantry of Irishmen in France and Gallipoli was rigidly excluded ; the London Irish was refused the use of the word Irish until the matter was brought up in Parliament." Rightly or wrongly it was firmly believed in Ireland that this deplorable action was due to the racial and religious bigotry of two men in the War Office,

The Blackest Ingratitude.

The Irish Future

Lord Kitchener and that brilliant and genial Irishman, Sir Henry Wilson, whose forefathers, like nearly all of his name in Ulster, may have abandoned their patronymic of O'Neil at the point of the British bayonet.

The exclusion of any mention of Irish gallantry at Gallipoli was a singularly utter baseness. Two regiments, the Dublin Fusiliers and the Munster Fusiliers bore the brunt of the attack at V Beach, according to official reports, " the most important " and " the most strongly defended of all " the six beaches, chosen for the landing of the troops in boats. In less than five minutes the boats were drifting about helplessly filled with dead and wounded," after superhuman efforts, in which hundreds of Irishmen laid down their lives. For years the War Office concealed the glorious truth.

The myriad tales of personal ill-usage told in Ireland by returned soldiers, often wounded, were probably, indeed certainly, exagger-

Personal Ill-usage. ated, but they were believed and they no doubt had a basis of reality. I may mention one which I heard from a reliable military authority, though I cannot vouch for it, having no means of inquiry or verification. It is to the effect that a battalion of the Munster Fusiliers, the Hero Regiment of Mons, was believed to be largely infected by Sinn Fein propaganda. It was broken up into companies, roundly a hundred men each, which were sent to a dozen different British regiments. It is easy to imagine the hot

reception they got from the English soldiers,—
kicking and cuffing was the least of it, and it is
not easy to blame the latter. If the story is true
the War Office was terribly unwise, and Ireland
suffered cruelly from the passion engendered. It
was such folly that made conscription impossible.

At the time the War broke out I had been for
a couple of years the official Liberal Candidate
for the Northern Division of Hampshire, which
included the great military head-quarters of
Aldershot, and had ample opportunity of witnessing the loyal enthusiasm not only of the regular
Irish Regiments, like the Munsters,
Connaughts, and Dublin Fusiliers, but   Loyal
Enthusiasm.
of "Redmond's Army," who were
encamped to the number of 10,000 within a few
miles from our home at Eversley. I spoke on
many recruiting platforms, but soon came to
know that things were going badly for Irishmen.

Mr. Winston Churchill's *Aftermath*, in many
ways a singularly honest book, recognises the
folly and wickedness of Lord   "Pitiless War
Kitchener's policy, but tries to ex-   onTortured
People."
cuse it solely by reference to the
civil rebellion of 1798, over a century ago. Irishmen are often blamed for their long memories of
ancient grievances and Cromwellian devilries, but
the War Office in 1914 had absolutely no justification for its vindictive reminiscences. Its action
was rank Orangeism and Toryism of the most

hateful kind. In 1916 there came the madcap rebellion, in which less than 1,000 men were concerned. It is absurd to blame England for the drum-head executions that followed, but what was wholly infamous was the manner in which Martial Law, quite justly proclaimed, degenerated into wholesale outrage in every corner of Ireland. That was not the fault of the English people, but entirely of Dublin Castle. Sir Horace Plunkett in the columns of *The Times* told a part of the tale. Mr. Erskine Childers, an English ex-officer, resident in Dublin, the son of a British Cabinet Minister, gave more details in the *Daily News* in four articles on " Military Rule in Ireland "—(*i*) " What it Means "; (*ii*) " What it means to Women "; (*iii*) " Looting "; and (*iv*) " Sabotage and Terror,"—one more painful than another. He summarised the position in these words : " An organised war was in steady and pitiless operation for *two and a half years* before it began, early in 1919, to provoke violent reprisals from amongst this tortured people against the agents of the Executive." *The Press censorship concealed these facts in 1916-19.* They were shameful. It was the rough, occasionally gross, house searches by night, particularly offensive to women, that made the Sinn Feiners see red. This was long before the arrival of the first Black and Tan from Scotland Yard. Outrage soon progressed to murder, arson, and other developments of the " Tiger qualities of an Imperial Race."

How many Englishmen are aware that, in the

The Irish Future

one week following the opening of the Northern Parliament by His Majesty King George, 188 homes of Belfast Catholics went up in flames and, as Sir Nevil Macready, the Chief of the Irish Police, very truly said, retaliation " is only human." Ten thousand Catholic men, hundreds of them ex-soldiers, who had fought for England, were driven out of Belfast, and wandering over the southern counties, in spite of protests by Catholic politicians and priests, laid in ashes the stately homes of the heirs of the Cromwellian settlers. Revenge may be human, but since the day of Cain it has rightly been denounced as devilish. Meanwhile it is horribly true, as a distinguished American put it, " I would rather be a nigger in the streets of New York than a Catholic in the streets of Belfast."

A Nigger in New York.

Things went from bad to worse till in the beginning of 1921 Mr. Asquith (Earl of Oxford), ex-Prime Minister, declared that " Things are being done in Ireland, with the knowledge and approval, if not under the direction of Government officials, which would disgrace the blackest annals of the lowest despotism in Europe." Lord Robert Cecil emphasised this statement in these words. " These crimes amounted to organised arson and organised murder by agents of the Crown. Murders were organised in the most brutal way. All that had been stated by some of the judicial officers of the Crown in Ireland." The Right Honble. C. F.

"Lowest Despotism."

The Irish Future

Masterman said : "Speaking with a full sense of my responsibility as former Cabinet Minister, I declare the evidence is overwhelming that a systematic policy of terror is being pursued in Ireland—defended by Lloyd George, backed up by the flagrant lies of Sir Hamar Greenwood and organised by officials in high places in Dublin." General Hugh Gough, an Irish hero of the War, at one time an Orange extremist, shocked by what he witnessed, wrote to the Press that "law and order have given place to a brutal anarchy, in which the armed agents of the Crown violate every law in aimless and vindictive and insolent savagery."

The prominent feature, indeed, in this whole business is that the charge of complicity, if not of active guidance of outrage by the British Government, was made by Englishmen of the most distinguished positions and highest worth. Lord Wimborne, Lord-Lieutenant of Ireland, made the following amazing statements in the House of Lords on the 20th June, 1918. They describe the preparations made by Sir Hamar Greenwood in order to safeguard his *régime* of terrorism from authoritative witnesses and from possible legal interference. The ex-Viceroy more than suggests that the " German Plot " was made in London. " Amid much that is obscure in the present Irish situation, one new fact stands out in the public eye. The innovation to which I refer is the change in the personnel of the Irish Executive.

Government Complicity.

The Irish Future

This change is not confined to the office of Lord-Lieutenant or Chief Secretary, but extends to other functionaries as well. It includes the high offices of Lord Chancellor of Ireland, Lord Chief Justice of Ireland, Commander of the Forces in Ireland, and its ramifications go further, into offices both great and small, even down to simple colonels and private secretaries. And it is to be remarked,—I think it is, if I may say so, somewhat unfortunate,—*that this new change has had the effect of removing from the Irish Government all, or nearly all, of those of professed sympathy with the cause of Irish nationality and most of those, I believe, who profess the Catholic faith.* In fact, the change in the personnel has been of so sweeping and dramatic a character that I think we are entitled to ask His Majesty's Government what this change portends.

"For what purpose have you fashioned this new Executive instrument? It is true that in partial explanation, at any rate, the Government have alleged the existence of a German plot in Ireland. One would like to know a little more about it. It is somewhat strange, in view of the highly specialised means of obtaining information which have recently existed in Ireland, that *neither I, nor, as far as I am aware, any other member of the late Irish Executive, was aware of the existence of this plot until it was discovered by the British Government in London.*"

It is difficult to find words of sufficient vigour and anger to denounce the guilty action thus ascribed to the Government by this Great Official, the Viceroy, the personal representative of His Majesty the King-Emperor. The infamy of the "alleged German plot" almost passes belief. Sir Hamar Greenwood certainly earned his peerage, though the Government hesitated eight years before presenting this ornament of civilization to the Upper House.

I must not overlook the fact that *The Times*, the highest representative of English opinion, commented, in a leading article of the 29th January, 1921, in these words :

"Simple Truth" from The Times.

"It is the simple truth that, confronting a very serious predicament in Ireland last summer, the Government had recourse to desperate methods. They may, indeed, have been well advised to create a body of young and courageous ex-officers to supplement the Irish police forces, for the ordinary resources of the Executive had failed ; but in no circumstances, however grave, was it pardonable for them to institute a force of irregulars under conditions which would have strained the discipline of even the most tried *personnel*, and to launch it upon the monstrous understanding that it was to be a law unto itself. No other British Government had ever sought to divest themselves of responsibility for the actions of their own servants. In attempting to do so, this Government betrayed the highest traditions of the British nation. *Deeds have unquestionably been done by them in Ireland which have lastingly*

The Irish Future

disgraced the name of Britain. British processes of justice, which for centuries have commanded the admiration of the world, have been supplanted by those of lynch law. *There have been indiscriminate burnings, pillagings, and shootings,* with what discernible results? A hatred of this country on the part of the Irish people that will last for generations, the binding together of the guilty and the innocent by ties of common suffering, and that frenzy of despair which even now inspires the Irish Volunteers to stand at bay."

This admirable vindication of British justice was, no doubt, due to the influence of the great Irishman, Lord Northcliffe.

Those, who foolishly chortle with a great joy at the idea of having successfully side-tracked the Irish Nation, may meditate with advantage on the following para- **England's Best Customer.** graphs from an article by Mr. Sidney Brooks, the well-known writer, in *The Sunday Times* of the 2nd January, 1921 :

" Probably few people are aware that Ireland is Great Britain's best customer. Ireland buys from our manufacturers or through our merchants more British goods, raw materials, and commodities than any other country in the world. We in turn depend upon Ireland for the supply of some of our most essential foodstuffs. Figures show the surely not inconsiderable fact that the value of British exports to Ireland was, roughly, two-thirds of the value of British exports to all the British dominions throughout the Empire."

The Irish Future

" There is a further and in some ways a stronger argument for peace to be found in the study of Irish exports to Great Britain. If few realise that Ireland is Great Britain's best customer, still fewer are aware of the extent to which we rely upon Ireland for our supplies of food."

The total value of the great trade between England and Ireland in 1918 was £320,000,000. **Great Trade.** This was not a normal year but the last before the Anglo-Irish Peace, for which we have statistics. These facts and figures at least indicate what a vast market lies at the door of Great Britain, which her " insane policy of terrorism " well nigh destroyed. Since the Treaty in 1922 the British Government has entirely neglected Southern Ireland and given no help, whilst it has poured out money in Ulster in support of the ephemeral policy of Partition and to maintain a military police of excessive strength.

CHAPTER V

THE IRISH IN THE UNITED STATES

(i) " Expressing thanks for their hospitable reception, Mr. Kellogg said the Irish Free State would have a big part to play in the future of the Nations."—

Daily Mail, 4th September, 1928.

(ii) " Indeed America is much more Irish than English people are apt to conceive. *The great majority* of the white population in America is of Irish descent. It is the Irish element that has long governed the politics of the Union."—

The Times, in 1863.

(iii) " It is the plain fact that it is Irish discontent, which now more than anything else blocks and must block a close understanding between the American and British democracies. . . . If it is true, as seems inconvertible, that for the future welfare of the world nothing is so essential as the maintenance of harmony between Great Britain and the United States then it is purely lamentable that the sore Irish should be suffered to continue running."—

The Times, July, 1922.

COMING from the Chief Official of the great Republic of the United States of America, the first of these statements made in Dublin a few months ago may move the vanity of many Irishmen, but I confess it fills me with anxiety. If

Free State Influence. its outlook were really confined to the Irish Free State, it would not be a prophecy of much moment, but it is more than probable that Mr. Kellogg, himself of Irish origin, had in mind not the few millions in the South of Ireland but the great Irish population across the Atlantic, which never has forgotten and never will forget its motherland. I do not suggest that this great nationality will fail in its loyalty to the land of its adoption, but that loyalty to the star-spangled banner and to Ireland may follow the same or parallel lines. In this outlook there is ground for anxiety and room for rare political sagacity. It is pathetic to observe in recent English political literature an utter ignorance of the Irish question and its manifest developments in the present and in the future. Even intellectual publications in London, like *The New Statesman* of the 24th November, 1928, are so crudely ill-informed about both hemispheres as to preface an article on world politics by the incredibly silly remark that " Ireland has ceased to be a factor of any importance in English affairs." One of the objects of this book is to show that the contrary is the fact.

Turning to the second quotation at the top of this chapter, it seems a most re-

"Merciless Rancour." markable thing to find the leading journal of Great Britain nearly three-quarters of a century ago stating that the " great

majority " of the American population was of
" Irish descent." But a still more remarkable
fact is that *The Times* knew what it was writing
about and was entirely accurate. It was known
and appreciated in England in those days that
the original English settlers of the seventeenth
and early eighteenth centuries had not increased
and multiplied very much. Their number was
never very large, and it was greatly depleted by
the emigration of many thousands of families of
English origin to Canada and to England during
the five years of the War of Independence from
1763-68. There is no doubt but that they were
treated with great cruelty and even brutality by
the American population, who could not forget
the very numerous massacres of American families
by the Indian allies of the English armies. There
was no condemnation of these abominations by
the English authorities and bills for scalps were
certainly presented by the Indians and possibly
paid. General FitzPatrick writing to his brother,
Lord Upper Ossory, in 1777 said, " The army is
exasperated to the most violent degree and seems
to consider laying the whole country waste and
extirpating the inhabitants as the only means of
putting an end to the work." Mr. Percy Greg's
History of the United States at page 229 denounces
the horrible maltreatment of the royalists of
British descent. " The merciless rancour of the
insurgents towards their loyal countrymen from
first to last was the disgrace of the American cause
and people, It reflects deep discredit on Congress,

which never attempted to restrain it." Flogging
and tarring and worse were common. The British
authorities kept up this insane alliance with the
red skins for half a century. Mr. T. C. Smith,
Professor of History, Massachusett's University,
in his *Wars between England and America,* states
that " As late as 1812 the British General Brock
entered into an alliance with the Shawnee Chief,
Tecumseh, and the nameless horrors of Indian
massacre and torture surged along the American
settlements on the Kentucky and Ohio frontiers,"

It is difficult to realise nowadays how intense
the hatred of the Colonists against the British
was on account of these deplorable

**Burning of
Washington.** occurrences, and the number of immigrants from England to the States
during the half-century following the recognition
of the Union as an independent nation was very
small. The War of 1812 and the burning of
Washington by British troops naturally did not
increase goodwill or aid immigration from England. The growth of industry and manufactures
in Great Britain itself absorbed British labour in
most profitable occupations. The misguided
action of the British Cabinet, under Palmerston
and Gladstone, during the War of Secession in
1862-65, added fuel to the fire. Even down to
the present day popular newspapers and popular
orators of undoubtedly British origin wax furious
at the ill-will shown by the English Government
to the Northern States, whilst the Southern Confederacy was hardly less bitter against the nation

that failed to succour them and, as they put it, betrayed them in the hope of injuring the States, both north and south. This is the chief cause of the hostility, almost inexplicable to an Englishman, which American historians have shown till very recent times. It is not too much to say that for a century after Washington founded the great American Republic, that is roundly down to 1875, the enormous growth of the American population owed little to England and the " Anglo-Saxons " sent no appreciable contingent. Indeed, the English element in the population, found mostly in the Southern States, suffered a considerable diminution due to the loss of many thousands of soldiers in the War of Secession.

A very curious practice has grown up amongst recent American writers and professors of classing all Irishmen, who are not Catholic, as Anglo-Saxon or Scoto-Irish. It **The Scoto-Irish.** is true that perhaps the largest element in the Irish emigration during the period before the Union of Great Britain and Ireland in 1800 was derived from the North of Ireland, sturdy Presbyterian farmers, who were driven from their homes by the greed of the great landlords of the Episcopal faith. This large contingent was wholly innocent of any admixture of British blood. The mass of the population had remained Irish, though they were forced to abandon their Catholic faith and usually also their Irish names. The great clan of O'Neil took the names of Macneill, Nelson, and Wilson. They were the landless labourers of the new Ulster settlers, whom they followed to America in great numbers.

Many estimates of the number of Irish in the United States have been made, but little that can be called statistics exists before the official census of 1890, which returned the number of Irish then living in the States, but born in Ireland, as 1,871,000, whilst those born in the States of Irish parents was 4,900,000. It was also officially estimated that, excluding these two classes, there were at that time roundly 20,000,000 persons " of Irish descent," or nearly 27,000,000 including them. These are strictly official figures. The total population was then, 63,000,000, which goes far to establish a considerable degree of accuracy in the statement of *The Times* in 1863 that " the great majority of the white population in America is of Irish descent." There is, indeed, authentic evidence of early settlements by Irishmen in all the Eastern States on the Atlantic. In 1689 the O'Carrolls came to Maryland and founded Carrolltown. In 1715 other Irish founded the new towns of Palmer and Worcester in Massachusetts. In 1723 the O'Sullivans built Belfast in Maine and a body of 4,000 came to Newcastle. In 1729, 6,000 settled in Philadelphia and formed the nucleus of the great Irish colony there, which now numbers hundreds of thousands. Williamsburg in South Carolina and many townlets in Virginia owed their existence to Irish immigration.

Professor Lecky, Conservative M.P. for Trinity

6,771,000 Irish and sons of Irish in 1890.

The Irish Future

College, Dublin, in his *History of England in the Eighteenth Century*, states that : "Already," in 1775, "the many disastrous circumstances of Irish history had driven great bodies of Irishmen to seek a home in America." The tide has flowed ever since. Besides 4,000,000 in Ireland there are over 2,000,000 of Irish in Great Britain, and as many more in Australia, Canada, and New Zealand. There is, therefore, it would seem probable, a population of at least 30,000,000 owing its origin to Ireland as its Motherland, much larger than any of the smaller nationalities in Europe and, indeed, approximating to those of some of the greater nations of the world, such as Italy and France. The Irish are singularly prolific, especially amidst the prosperity of the United States. The Convent drums it into the Irish girl's head that motherhood is the glory of woman and a God-guided duty. I may mention that in the *Nineteenth Century* for May, 1910, Mr. W. S. Lilly stated, without criticism, that "over 40,000,000 inhabitants of the United States have a share of Irish blood from one parent or another."

It is not too much to say that the Revolution of 1763, whilst it owed much of its origin to the liberty-loving ideals of English Puritans, owed its success to Irish soldiers. Lecky points out that the famous Pennsylvanian Line, the best regiments in Washington's army, were almost entirely made up of Northern Irish, whilst of the remainder of

109

his troops it is claimed that 38 per cent. were Southern Irish. In the British Parliament it was stated, on the report of the British generals on the spot, that over half of the whole army were Irish. The most striking proof of the Irish and Catholic origin of the greater part of Washington's victorious army is the astonishing fact that immediately after the Declaration of Independence a public service of thanksgiving was held in Philadelphia, then the Capital of the New Republic. It took the form of a High Mass, sung in the Old Church of St. Mary on the 4th July, 1779, in the presence of all the members of Congress, led by " the President, the official heads of the New Government, the Officers of the Army and Navy and the French and Spanish Ministers." An even more startling fact is that on the 4th November, 1781, " following the surrender of the British under Cornwallis to Washington at Yorktown another solemn mass of thanks was said and *the conquered flags of Great Britain were laid upon the altar steps* " of this Catholic church in recognition of the supreme services rendered by the Irish, who at Yorkstown formed 75 per cent. of the American Forces. The above quotations are from a tablet on the north side of the old church.

The United States and especially New York are in a singular degree indebted to the Irish race, whose services to her greatness began **Thomas Dongan.** long, long ago. How many Americans remember that it was to a Catholic Irishman that New York owed its first parlia-

ment? Mr. Roosevelt in his admirable monograph on the capital city writes : " Thomas Dongan, the first Governor, a Catholic Irish gentleman
of good family, the nephew of the Earl of Tyrconnell, acted with wise liberality both in matters
political and in matters religious, towards the
province he was sent to govern, for he was a man
of high character and good capacity. He was
also vigilant in preserving order and warding off
outside aggression and, devoted to the well-being
of the Colony, he proved himself perhaps the
best colonial Governor New York ever had.
Dongan reached New York in 1683 and from the
first was popular with the colonists. He at once
issued writs for the election of the members of
the long desired Provincial Assembly. With its
meeting the province took the first real step—
and a very long one—towards self-government."

A very authoritative observer and distinguished
journalist, Mr. A. G. Gardiner, a couple of years
ago, after a prolonged tour through
the States, emphasised the argument **The Seats of the Mighty.**
in these words : " *Consider the facts.*"
The Irish " form the most solid and formidable
political mass in the country. They are formidable, not so much because of their great
numbers, as because they are the one political
body moving with a single idea in a compact
mass through the life of the nation. They are
not socially negligible. *They are in the Seats of
the Mighty.*" To instance a few, there are Judges
by the dozen, including a third of the Supreme

111

Court, three Cardinals, Senators, multi-millionaires
and captains of industry by the score, like Mr.
Henry Ford, the motor King, Mr. Doheny, who
dominates the petrol industry at the present time,
Mr. Thomas F. Ryan, the partner of King Leopold
in the Congo diamond mines, Mr. Choate, the
ex-Ambassador to London, Mr. Mellon, the Secretary to the Treasury, Mr. Dougherty, the Attorney-
General, Mr. Smith, the Governor of New York,
Mr. Hylan, the Mayor of New York, Mr. Tumulty,
recently Private Secretary to President Wilson,
General O'Ryan, who organized the American
Army in the War, Dudley Malone, the Chief Official
of the Port of New York, J. F. Ryan, the head
of the Copper Trust, John Mitchell, son of the
famous Irish rebel of 1848, and Mayor of New
York, W. H. Mahoney, Manager, Foreign Trade
Bureau of New York, Colonel Concannon, Chairman of the White Star Line, J. A. Farrell, President U.S. Steel Co., and Mr. Hurley, who carried
out, during the War, the great ship and dock
building, which added some 8,000,000 tons to
the U.S. Mercantile Marine. Few of these gentlemen have ever shown any affection for the land
of their origin and are even ashamed of it, but
they are of Irish origin and the fact tells. The
Irish are none too proud of some of them. " The
most brilliant writers on the Press are Irish.
Nearly every political caucus is under Irish control. Most of the great cities have Irish mayors.
The police are almost invariably Irish. *The Irish
vote is the crucial element of every election.* No

candidate, whether for a mayoralty, a State governorship, the Senate or the Presidency, can ignore it."

At the recent election for the Presidency of the United States as many as 16,000,000 votes were cast for Mr. Alfred L. Smith, the Irish Catholic candidate, or more than one-third of the total electorate. His defeat was chiefly due to the votes of women, who suspected him of anti-prohibition leanings, whilst the Southern States went mad over his papistry. These sources of hostility will be far less active in years to come.

CHAPTER VI

THE IRISH ON THE CONTINENT OF EUROPE

(i) " I cannot too highly esteem those gentlemen of Ireland who, with all the disadvantages of being exiles and strangers, have been able to distinguish themselves, in so many parts of Europe, by their valour and conduct ABOVE ALL OTHER NATIONS."

Dean Swift.

(ii) " In wide Christendom what race can emulate the extraordinary fact that during the second half of last century, the glorious nineteenth, three Irishmen, all of them Catholics, ruled three of the great nations of the world for long periods? From 1873 to 1879 Marshal Patrick MacMahon, Duke of Magenta, as President, saved France from the miseries of German conquest and of internal communism. Similarly for eleven years Count Taaffe of Roscommon, Imperial Chancellor of the Austro-Hungarian Empire, held that great State together, when shaken almost to pieces by the German victories of 1866. Was it not a dirty thing to deprive the son of this distinguished man,—and a good friend of England too,— of his Irish peerage, because he fought for the land that gave a home to his Catholic ancestors when driven from Ireland by religious bigotry? The third of the wonderful trio of great statesmen was Marshal Leopold O'Donnell, Duke of Tetuan, who as Prime Minister of Spain for eight

His Excellency Charles O'Donnell, Duke of Tetuan,
President of the Senate at Madrid.

years, from 1860 to 1868, kept his sovereign on the throne
in days of revolution and laid the foundations on which
the restored monarchy has since been built up."—

The Lordship of the World.
page 139.

(iii) "At home they had sunk into torpid and degraded
pariahs" as the result of three centuries of grinding
oppression.—

W. E. Lecky
*History of England in
the Eighteenth Century.*

THERE is an almost forgotten shrine of the Irish
Race in Rome that might form the centre and
inspiration of a great Irish National
Resurrection.   No more holy spot   A Forgotten
Shrine.
exists in wide Christendom, outside
the Holy Land, than the site which Pope Pius V
gave as a last resting place for the dethroned
Irish Princes who were finally broken in 1608
and driven from their homes and territories by
the largest army England ever put into the field
—larger than that which carried the leopards of
England all over France two centuries before.
How little do Englishmen, and even Irishmen,
appreciate the great fact of Irish history that as
late as the beginning of the seventeenth century
Irish princes, the O'Neil and the O'Donnell, the
direct descendants of the ancient kings of all
Ireland, were monarchs over Ulster and had held

115

back for four hundred years the English armies that began the conquest of Ireland by Henry II in 1172.

In front of the high altar of the Church of San Pietro in Montorio, at the very spot where Catholic tradition relates that St. **Tombstones of Princes.** Peter, the first Pope, was crucified head downwards, stand the tombstones of Princeps O'Neil and Princeps O'Donnell, the Latin inscriptions on which record how these great noblemen fought together for faith and fatherland and all that brave men hold most dear. Very few Irishmen, so great has been modern Irish degradation, find their way to this national shrine. American Irish seem never to have heard of its existence. Shabby shoneen Dublin has not a single street or square called after Shan O'Neil or Hugh O'Donnell. As to Englishmen, Ireland has found them singularly ungenerous foemen. They rightly revere the memories of every patriot from William Wallace to Andreas Höfer, but have never a word of kindliness or admiration for the noble Irish families, who sacrificed everything, except honour, for the homesteads of their people and the altars of their God, and then went forth to every land in Europe to raise the Irish name to undying fame. After such supreme suffering no nation has a higher claim to adopt as its National Anthem the verses of a brilliant Irishman.

" I vow to thee my country,—all earthly things above,—

116

The Irish Future

Entire and whole and perfect, the service of my
    love,
The love that asks no question : the love that stands
    the test,
That lays upon the altar the dearest and the best :
The love that never falters, the love that pays
    the price,
The love that makes undaunted the final sacrifice."

England may yet learn to recognise and honour
the myriads of Irishmen, who for love of country
through the centuries laid " upon the altar the
dearest and the best."

I often wonder if it is possible to reawaken
in Irish breasts that pride of race that for centuries kept alive a noble patriotism
and, what is even more important, **Pride of Race.**
a high courage and an indigenous
civilisation. In the history of conquering peoples
there is no page more base than that which tells
of the destruction of the Irish nobility and of
Irish education. The persistent burning of old
records and of ancient literature simply wiped
out every genealogy and every trace of family
history. Every school went up in flames and Irish
youth found education only behind the hedges
or on the hillside. The following pages are intended to open up again the ancient outlook. I
would urge my countrymen to cultivate an intense
pride in their world-wide race, to drop their
ignorant veneration for shoddy and un-Irish
revolutionaries, like Wolfe Tone and Parnell, and

to bear in loving memory Red Hugh O'Donnell and Owen Roe O'Neill, Rury O'Moore and Cahir O'Doherty, O'Connell and O'Carroll, Tyr Owen and Tyr Hugh. That Parnell was an undesirable is admitted, but he was preferable to the arch-anarchist, Wolfe Tone, who in his *Autobiography* records these two unattractive opinions:

(i) " The Pope is dethroned and in exile. I hope this is but the beginning of his sorrows. Many a long century he and his predecessors have been fleecing all Europe."

(ii) " I should have rejoiced to have battered down the gates of the Convent. These Convents are most infernal institutions."

Irishmen in the service of France, ranging from an Earl of Tyrconnell, French Ambassador at Berlin in 1752, to an O'Neil, Field-Marshal and War Minister under Napoleon III in 1869, are so very numerous that it would be no easy task to mention even their names. The Irish Brigade in Louis XIV's reign numbered at times as many as 30,000 men, and its historians claim that nearly half a million of Irishmen passed through its ranks in the eighteenth century. M. de la Pouce, a French military historian, alleges that " as the result of researches in the archives of the Department of War it has been proved that between the years 1650 and 1800 more than 750,000 Irishmen gave their lives for the glory of France (*à l'éclat du nom Français*)." It is to be feared that these brave men gained nothing but glory for them-

" 750,000 Irishmen gave their lives."

selves and their country. They were underpaid and often half starved, whilst, as at Fontenoy, they were given tasks and called on to win or defend posts which involved certain slaughter. Their commanders were men like Lieutenant-General Lord Maguire of Enniskillen, Lieutenant-General Count Arthur Dillon, General Count Daniel O'Mahony, General Pierce Butler, Lord Galmoy, General the Earl of Tyrconnell, General Lord O'Farrell of Annaly, General Lord Dunsany, General Count Charles O'Gara, General Count Daniel O'Donnell, Patrick Sansfield, Earl of Lucan, Chevalier Count Patrick Darcy, General O'Brien, Viscount Clare, Donough MacCarthy, Earl of Clancarty, Lord Mountcashel, General William Lord Blakeney of Limerick, and scores of others, O'Ryans, Fitzgeralds, O'Neils, Burkes, Murphys and Barrys, Generals and Colonels.

The ancient family of Kavenagh, overlords of the Province of Leinster, one of whose princes invited Henry II to the Conquest of Ireland, gave a very distinguished **Dictator of France.** son to the service of France in the middle of the nineteenth century, General Louis Eugène Cavaignac, who, as Minister of War and practically Dictator of France, suppressed the Paris insurrection of 1848. He was the popular candidate for the Presidency of the French Republic and received a million and a half votes against five and a half millions recorded for Napoleon III.

An even more distinguished son of Ireland is

The Irish Future

M. Aristide Briand, the Breton, who has been twelve times Prime Minister of France, and to-day her most eloquent and successful Minister for Foreign Affairs. His wonderful tact and sincere desire for goodwill has made him the most powerful influence in Europe for international peace. Mr. T. P. O'Connor has stated that a great bond between himself and his French friend is that they are not only brother Celts, but that the latter's great-grand father, Conal Brien, came from Ireland.

Twelve Times Prime Minister.

Probably the most chivalric personality of Irish origin was Count Thomas Lally, Baron de Tolendal, who attended as aide-de-camp the Young Pretender, Prince Charles Edward in Scotland. He was created General by Louis XV after the battle of Fontenoy in 1744 and in 1756 appointed Governor of Pondicherri. His famous attack on British power in India and his subsequent betrayal by the French Government is one of the saddest episodes of military history. His title of Tolendal is a French translation of Tullagh-na-Daly, which means Daly's Hill, in County Galway.

France's Irish General in India.

No Irishman, except perhaps Wellington, has filled a more exalted position in Europe than Marshal Patrick Marie MacMahon, Duc de Magenta. His great services as President of the French Republic are matters of modern history and that she survived in undiminished power to fight Germany a second time is mainly due to his

A Great Gentleman.

The Irish Future

extraordinary influence amongst men of different political views and his patriotic teaching of the supreme need of union amongst all of them for their country's sake. There never was an act more becoming in a great gentlemen than his letter to General Mantenfiel on the termination of the occupation by the German Army. It was dated the 4th September, 1873, and said : " I deem it my duty to express to its Commander-in-Chief the sentiments which I experience on account of the justice and impartiality shown by him in the difficult mission which was entrusted to him." The Germans had in fact acted with splendid magnanimity to their defeated enemy, very different from the unclean brutality of the French in the Rhineland and Ruhr in 1918.

Henry James Clarke, Duc de Feltre and Marshal of France, was a distinguished General and especially pre-eminent amongst the Marshals of the Great Napoleon for **An Organiser of Victory.** his administrative and organising genius. He was first appointed Secretary for War in 1804, but returned to the field the following year, becoming Governor of Vienna and taking over charge of the great city and of several surrounding provinces from the Austrian Governor, Count Andrew O'Reilly. He was Governor of Berlin in 1807. Clarke's chief claim to fame is that from 1807 to 1814, the period of Napoleon's greatest military activity and glory, he was Minister of War at Paris. He was created a peer of France in 1814. Irishmen in the service of Austria were a glorious company and merit an admiring recognition, even in England. Colonel W. O. Cavenagh **Irish Generals in Austria.** has given, in the *Journal* of the Royal Society of Antiquaries of Ireland, a full account of these distinguished soldiers. No doubt, the most prominent sprang from the ancient Ulster family of O'Donnell. I have given details of their great services in the Memoir which forms the last chapter of this book. Their names were :—

(i) General Count Charles O'Donnell, born in Ireland in 1715, Grand Cross of the Order of Maria Theresa—the equivalent of the V.C. of England ; Governor of the Netherlands in 1762.

(ii) Field-Marshal Count John O'Donnell, Grand Cross of the Order of Maria Theresa.

(iii) Major-General Count Henry O'Donnell, born in Mayo in 1726, Grand Cross of the Order of Maria Theresa.

(iv) Count Joseph O'Donnell, Finance Minister, President of the Upper House and Governor of Carinthia.

(v) Field-Marshal Count Maurice O'Donnell.

(vi) Count Maximilian O'Donnell, aide-de-camp to the Emperor Franz Josef, whose life he saved in 1852.

Others were as great.

Field-Marshal Count Francis Maurice Lacy of Ballingarry, County Limerick, a most distinguished commander and from 1766 **Field Marshals Galore.** to 1778 War Minister and President of the War Council at Vienna.

Field-Marshal Count Ulysses Browne of Moyne,

County Mayo, Governor of Transylvania and Austrian General in Silesia against the Great Frederick, who spoke of him as his teacher in the art of war. He was Colonel-in-Chief of the 36th Bohemian Infantry, which bore his name down to 1918, when the Czechoslovak Republic arose.

Field-Marshal Count Laval Nugent, nephew of the first Earl of Westmeath, born at Ballingar in 1777. He fought Napoleon's armies from 1793 to 1815 and was given the honorary rank of Lieutenant-General in the British Army and K.C.B. He was created a Prince of the Holy Roman Empire and a Magnate of Hungary. He married the Duchess Riario-Sforza, co-heiress of Francis Xavier, Prince of Poland and Saxony.

Major-General Count Oliver Walsh of Carrighmayne (Carrickmines), County Dublin, created a Baron by the Emperor Ferdinand III, Imperial Chamberlain. It is interesting to note that his descendant, Baron Oliver Carrighmayne, commanded a brigade of cavalry at Königgrätz in 1866.

Field-Marshal Count George Oliver Walsh, eldest son of the above, Governor of Messina in Italy, and Generalissimo of the Austrian Army in Turkey, Knight of the Polish White Eagle.

General Count John Sigismund Maguire of Lurg, County Fermanagh, Governor of Carinthia and Grand Cross of the Order of Maria Theresa.

General Count Richard Dalton of Grenanstown, County Tipperary, General Commanding in the Netherlands, 1778-1799.

The Irish Future

General Baron John Baptist Purcell, commanding in Slavonia in 1779, and related to the Spanish-Irish family of Merry del Val.

General Baron Thomas Brady of Cootehill, County Cavan, Governor of Dalmatia and Privy Councillor to the Emperor.

Colonel Count William O'Mahony of Dunlo Castle, Kerry, killed in 1805 at Bassano, fighting against the French under Masséna.

Major-General Baron John O'Brien, Count Thomond, held many commands against the Generals of Napoleon.

General Count Andrew O'Reilly of Ballinlough, County Westmeath, distinguished himself in the Italian campaigns and commanded a cavalry brigade at Austerliz; Governor of Vienna.

Field-Marshal Count Philip Magawly of Kilcormac, Kings County, Count Cerati in Bavaria, descended from Awly Macaulay, to whom Queen Elizabeth wrote a letter, addressed to " our well beloved cousin, chief of his clan and lord of his nation," Governor of Prague. His grand nephew was envoy from the Pope to Napoleon in 1812 and Prime Minister to the ex-Empress Maria Louisa. This family returned to Ireland and the Field-Marshal's great, great-grandson, Colonel Magawly de Calry, of the 15th Hussars, was killed at the battle of the Somme, when commanding a battalion of the Rifle Brigade. There can be little doubt but that the Great Duke of Wellington, the Marquis Wellesley and the Earls Cowley sprang from this ancient family. Their original name was Colley,

which is very common in County Down in its
earliest form of Cawley or MacAulay.

General Count John Joseph O'Dwyer of Kil-
namanagh, County Tipperary, appointed by the
Emperor Charles VI Governor of Belgrade. His
brother was a Russian Admiral and the Honble.
Sir Michael O'Dwyer, G.C.S.I., Governor of the
Punjab during the Great War, is of the same
family.

General Baron Patrick O'Neillan of Ballyally
Castle, Bunratty, County Clare.

Field-Marshal Francis Wenzil Walsh, of Carrighmayne, County Dublin, Count of the Holy Roman
Empire, commanding in Hungary, and Knight of
the Golden Fleece.

Colonel William Count Gall von Bourckh was,
the second son of Walter Gall Burke of Gallstown
County Kilkenny, one of five brothers, who lived
and died in the service of Austria. Baron Holstein
in Silesia.

General Caspar Count von Chavaignac, of a
Leinster family, who raised the cuirassier regiment
of Kavanagh for service in Hungary.

Field-Marshal Count Francis Taaffe, 3rd Earl
of Carlingford, born at Ballymote, County Sligo,
brought a regiment of 1,800 Irishmen to Austria,
Knight of the Golden Fleece, Prime Minister of
Lorraine and Governor of Nancy.

Lieutenant-General Baron Thomas Plunkett,
born in Kilkenny in 1716, a kinsman of Lord
Dunsany, Adjutant-General in the War of the
Spanish Succession and Governor of Antwerp.

The Irish Future

General Count William O'Kelly of Gallagh, County Galway, General Commanding at the Battle of Breslau, 1757.

Colonel Chevalier Hume Caldwell, third son of Sir James Caldwell, Bart., born on the shores of Lough Erne in 1735. Enlisting as private, he became Colonel of the Croatian contingent at many battles.

General Count James Macdonnell of Mayo, Imperial Chamberlain, died 1766. At the battle of Cremona he captured the French Marshal de Villeroy. Of the same family was Lord Macdonnell of Swinford in Mayo, recently a Governor in India and Under-Secretary of State in Dublin. The destruction, almost root and branch, of the Catholic branch of the Macdonnells, Earls of Antrim, is the most terrible incident of the Elizabethan wars in Ireland. In 1575 its head was Charles Macdonnell (Sorley Buy), who married a daughter of the O'Neil, Earl of Tyrone, and brought to the Irish army a large Scottish contingent. He paid a terrible price for his fidelity to his Irish relatives. He sent his wife and young son and some 600 women and children to the island of Rathlin, on the coast of Antrim, for safety. Sir John Norris, the English general, found out their retreat, and, landing a few men, had the whole party massacred. The Earl of Essex, writing to Queen Elizabeth, described how " Sorley then also stood upon the mainland of the Glynnes and saw the taking of the island, and was likely to run mad for sorrow, tearing and tormenting himself, as the spy sayeth,

and saying he had then lost all he ever had." The
Queen applauded this awful tragedy and wrote to
Essex, " Give the young gentleman, John Norrice,
the executioner of your well-devised enterprize,
to understand that we will not be unmindful of
his good services." A few survivors on the mainland escaped into Mayo.

In no country in Europe have men of the Irish
race won higher distinction than in Spain. At
the present day His Excellency the
Marquis Merry del Val, of an ancient **Great Irishmen in Spain.**
Connaught family, is the Ambassador
of Spain at the Court of St. James, whilst his
brother, the Cardinal Merry del Val, was very
recently Secretary or Foreign Minister at the
Vatican. Their father, His Excellency Don Rafael
Merry del Val, was Ambassador at Vienna.

Of equally great distinction in Spain is the
family of O'Donnell, Princes of Ulster and by
English creation Earls of Tyrconnell. The last
Earl was attainted in 1608, because, as the warrant
of attainder clearly states, he was in alliance with
the Spaniards, " *quia Hispanis adhaerens*," in
the last great struggle for Irish freedom, that ended
by the defeat in 1602 of the Spanish and Irish
armies at Kinsale, in County Cork. Amongst the
Irish nobility, who fled to Spain after the battle of
the Boyne in 1689 was Hugh O'Donnell of Murrisk
in County Mayo. He became a General in the
Spanish army and settled in Andalusia, from whom
in the fourth generation sprang Leopold O'Donnell,
Count de Lucana. He supported Queen Isabella

on the throne in 1843 and maintained her there for over a quarter of a century. In 1860 he conquered Morocco and was created Duke of Tetuan. Since the preceding year he had been Prime Minister and held that office nearly to his death, in 1868. His uncle, General Charles O'Donnell, Count La Bisbal, was Director-General of Artillery.

Major-General Richard Wall, born in Waterford in 1694, was more distinguished in civil than military employ and was Spanish Ambassador in London in 1747 and in 1754 became Foreign Minister at Madrid. He maintained a very friendly attitude to England.

Field Marshal Count Alexander O'Reilly, born in 1722 at Baltrasna in County Meath, had much to do with the formation of an Irish Brigade in Spain, consisting of the Regiments Hibernia, Irlanda and Ultonia (Ulster). The flag of the last has become the town flag of Gerona in Catalonia in remembrance of its magnificent defence of that city against the troops of Napoleon I. The 23rd Regiment of Spanish Infantry is still called *"Irlanda el Famoso."* He distinguished himself greatly at the battle of Hochkirchen in Prussia in 1758 and afterwards remodelled the Spanish army on Prussian lines. In 1768 he commanded a powerful force in America and captured Louisiana from the French. Later he commanded an expedition to Algiers and became Governor of Madrid and Captain-General of Andalusia.

Of less important Irish soldiers of fortune in Spain were General O'Ryan, one of the last

The Irish Future

Spanish Governors of Mexico, General O'Daly, General O'Doyle and General O'Farrell, Minister of War to Ferdinand VII, when the French, under Prince Murat, occupied Madrid in 1810. O'Daly afterwards became Portuguese Ambassador in Paris.

Although he gained his great military pre-eminence in the British Army, Field-Marshal James O'Hara, Baron Tyrawley and **The British Field-Marshal O'Hara.** Baron Kilmaine, did all his fighting on the Continent. Born in 1690, in Ireland, he began his service at the battle of Malplaquet under the great Marlborough, who regarded him as his ablest general. He received his second peerage at the age of thirty-two and was British Ambassador to Russia in 1741.

Several Irishmen arrived at the peerage in England, the Earl of Donoughmore, original name Healy; (ii) Earl of Listowel, Hare or O'Hehir; (iii) Lord de Tabley, **Irish Peers in England.** O'Byrne; (iv) Earl Cadogan, Corrigan; (v) Lord Lyndhurst, Copley or na Copall. The name of Manning, the Cardinal, is a modification of the Sligo Manion and the Smith family, from which the Earl of Birkenhead sprang, is said in Liverpool to have come, as is undoubtedly true of his name-sake in New York, from Ireland.

CHAPTER VII

THE GERMAN FRIENDS OF IRELAND

"**Armagh, the Educational Capital of Christian Ireland, was the metropolis of Civilization.**"—

Professor Darmesteter.

"**Ireland was regarded by all Europe as the principal centre of learning and piety. The Anglo-Saxons were the one of all nations which derived most profit from the teaching of the Irish Schools.**"—

Montalembert.

IT is with a grave shame that one must feel that there are few people with less pride in their origin than the Irish in the United States.

Race. Pride.

The Americans of English descent are, to their great honour, endued with the most vivid recognition of the great past of their race. They are always dinning into our ears its manifold excellencies, and I certainly honour them for their ancestral patriotism. I fear the Irish in America leave to others the exposition of their ancient and modern greatness.

One great bond between the Irish and Germans

130

in the United States is that both have been gratuitously attacked in the " Anglo-Saxon " policy of the Quota. These magnificent races are classed with the undesirables, whose immigration should be **"The Foundation of Civilization."** hampered, if not stopped. There are, however, ties far greater and far older than the ephemeral vindictiveness of to-day can call into existence. Very few Irishmen appreciate the boundless debt we owe to German scholarship and German goodwill. It is necessary to remind them that Ireland has an outstanding record for services to European civilisation. I do not refer to her having evangelised England, Scotland, and Germany, but to her wider educational activities, which radiated from the University of Armagh, the oldest in the world. During the revival of Celtic studies in the middle of last century, when Zeuss found in the ancient Irish speech the key to Indo-European languages, from Hindustan to Norway, the history of Early Ireland was first scientifically approached by Professor Zimmer of the University of Berlin. In his book on *The Irish Element in Mediaeval Culture* he summarised the work of Irish scholars in these words : " Ireland can indeed lay claim to a great past : she can not only boast of having been the birthplace and abode of high culture in the fifth and sixth centuries, at a time when the Roman Empire was being undermined by the alliances and inroads of German tribes, which threatened to sink the whole Continent into barbarism, but also of having made strenuous efforts in the seventh and *up to the tenth century* to spread her learning among the German and Romance peoples, thus forming the *actual foundation of our present Continental civilisation.*" Another German historian of this period, Darmesteter, **"The Asylum of the Higher Learning."** says : " The Renaissance began in Ireland 700 years before it was known in Italy. During 300 years Ireland was the asylum of the higher learning. Armagh, the educational capital of Christian Ireland, was *the metropolis of civilisation.*" Amongst French witnesses to these facts I may mention M. Haureau of the French Academy, who bore testimony in these words, " While the rest of the Roman world was imbruted by the fury of the barbaric conquest, the schools of Ireland remained intact and flourishing, and famous masters professed before a numerous youth not only the eloquence and poetry of Latium, but the grammar and philosophy of Greece." Montalembert says, " Ireland was re-garded by all Europe as the principal centre of learning and piety. . . . The mania of the Irish for Greek was even carried so far that they wrote the Latin of the Church books in Hellenic charac-ters." He added : " The Anglo-Saxons were the one of all nations which derived most profit from the teaching of the Irish schools."

That excellent Anglo-Saxon, Alfred the Great, received his education in Ireland, along with the sons of many another English King and Frankish princes from Paris and Cologne. The culture of

The Irish Future

Oxford and Cambridge, of Harvard and Yale, knows nothing of these things, but a reawakened Irish nation will republish them to the world and to all posterity.

The Germans have always formed a very large element in the North American population. As early as 1690 Jacob Leisler was the leader of the popular or Democratic Party in New York, " a merchant **The First Democratic Party.** of property and deacon of the Dutch Reformed Church " (Roosevelt), who gave his life for " Government by the people." He taxed the wealthy Dutch and English landlords for State improvements. Such conduct was clearly high treason and he was duly executed. Soon after, about 1720, Mr. Roosevelt states that there was a great influx of Germans from the Rhine Provinces. "They were poor peasants, who fled before the French armies." The terrible devastation and massacres by Louis XIV's troops in the end of the previous century had warned the people of the Palatinate and of the country surrounding Aix-la-Chapelle of the danger of living near the frontier of a merciless enemy. During the long reign of this King the whole of Western and Southern Germany was periodically ravaged by the most ruthless soldiery in Europe. America gained a very valuable population, almost entirely Catholic, which, like the early Irish, unserved by a Catholic priesthood, passed into the ranks of American Nonconformity, being attracted chiefly to the

Presbyterian community, which has always been the home of American freedom. Under the kindly protection of the followers of Penn they became the principal element in the population of Pennsylvania and made it the most orderly and prosperous State of the Union.

Mr. Roosevelt, in his admirable monograph of New York City, writes, pages 184-5, "The Germans had formed an important **German Swarms.** element of the city's population ever since the days of Leisler, with the exception of Stuyvesant, the most important figure in the history of the colonial town. They were probably in point of numbers and importance at no time lower than the fourth in rank among the nationalities that were being fused together to make New York citizens." "The new swarms of Germans who came hither," about 1820 and 1850 and after 1880, "revived the use of the German tongue; and, as they settled in large bodies—often forming the entire population of certain districts—they clung pertinaciously to their own customs, kept to their own churches, and published their own newspapers." "They were thrifty, hardworking and on the whole law-abiding, and they not only rose rapidly in the social scale but, as soon as they learned our language, they became undistinguishable from the other Americans with whom they mixed. They furnished leading men to all trades and professions and many founded families of high social and political distinction." According to the Census of 1880, there were 1,966,742 Germans in the States, who had been born in Germany. At the present time Americans of German origin, especially in the so-called Middle West, number 12,000,000, probably more, verily a population that deserves well of the Republic.

Although a large proportion of the Germanic immigrants were, including an Austrian contingent, Catholics, there was little community of feeling or politics between them and the Irish. The latter were democrats and pro-French, whilst the Teutonic races were Republican and pro-English. This segregation would have continued unbroken, but for the folly and, indeed, the malevolence of the old Americans during the Great War, when the persecuted and outraged Germans found their warmest defenders amongst Irish public men, who had known what it was to be maligned by the "Anglo-Saxon" Press in the States. If I were to venture on a prophecy in regard to the great German population in Northern America, I would venture to say that no section of the population is more ready to welcome the advent of a third party that would be at once democratic and free from racial bias. It had a terrible experience in the late War, when the cent.-per-cent. Anglo-Saxon newspapers vied with one another in portraying the German as lost to almost every sentiment of humanity, base and brutal in every international relation. I learned in Chicago that the number of Germans in that very German

Irish Defenders.

The Irish Future

neighbourhood driven into the asylums for the insane by ill-usage was painfully large. The Irishmen of New York will be wise in their generation if they whole-heartedly support the Germans and Swedes of Ohio and Minnesota, who are fighting for the rights of the farmer. It is a struggle that the Irish have already won, though under different circumstances. In Ireland it was the landlord who exceeded his rights. In the States it is the unjust capitalist, the trusts and monopolies that rig the prices of land and wheat and meat in one year to extravagant heights and in the next break them down below the cost of production. Germans and Irish should be intimate friends in America. The union of the cultures of Germany and Ireland would add a new dignity to the public life of the United States.

CHAPTER VIII

THE WAR MADNESS OF FRANCE

GERMANY PILLAGED THROUGH THREE CENTURIES

"Wishing to concentrate his chief efforts upon Italy and the Lower Rhine, Louis decided to evacuate the Palatinate, and, by the advice of Louvois, orders were given in December 1688 to devastate the country. Heidelberg was sacked in March 1689, and, shortly after, Mannheim, Speier, and Worms suffered a similar fate; Ladenberg and Oppenheim were burnt, and a large tract of country, including not only the Palatinate but parts of the Electorate of Trier and of the Margravate of Baden were also ravaged. The Rhine district was in great measure ruined."—

Cambridge Modern History,
vol. v, pp. 56-7.

"The towns were reduced to ashes, the inhabitants murdered or dragged into France. In Spires the Imperial vaults were broken open, and the remains of the Emperors desecrated."—

Menzel's *History of Germany*.

In the ordinary Englishman's mind the history of Europe seems to have begun in 1871, that is, at the end of the Franco-German War, when the infamous conquerors despoiled their gentle

How Alsace became a French Province. neighbour of the rich French provinces of Alsace and Lorraine, clearly an act particularly wicked and brutal. How many Englishmen know or remember how these provinces became part of France? The late Lord Bryce will be for most Englishmen a reliable witness to the truth. In his admirable essay, *The Holy Roman Empire*, he denounced their seizure in 1688 by Louis XIV as "robbery in time of peace which brought the monarchy of Louis nearer the heart of the German Empire." "His ambition and cruelty were witnessed to by repeated wars and the devastation of the Rhine countries." Another great Englishman, Sir James Stephen, in his *Lectures on French History*, describes French devilment at that time in the following awful passage : "Prodigal as the waste of treasure in the wars of Louis with the other

" Cold-blooded Crimes and Atrocities." powers of Europe was, history has a far darker tale of the utter ruin and desolation, by the armies of Louis, of the defenceless cities of Worms, Spires, and Oppenheim, of all the territories of Trèves and Baden, and of all the towns, villages, and hamlets of the Palatinate and of the unarmed inhabitants of those once smiling regions—crimes, which as they were wantonly perpetrated in cold blood and by one Christian and civilised people upon another, threw into the shade the worst ravages of Attila and Genseric and almost

challenged a comparison with the atrocities of the
day of St. Bartholomew "—by the way, another
French massacre. It was in such surroundings
that Elsass and Lothringen became two French
Provinces. As *Chambers's Encyclopædia*, with the
impartiality of fifty years ago, puts it : " Alsace
is exceedingly fertile, rich also in mines and
manufactures "—like the Ruhr Valley. " It fell
a prey to the aggressions of Louis XIV, who
seized Strassburg by surprise in time of peace.
Thus was this fine land and one of the noblest
branches of the race alienated from the German
people." Mr. Roosevelt, in his *History of New
York*, p. 87, mentions that " About 1720 there
was a great influx of Germans from the Rhine
Provinces. They were poor peasants, who had
fled before the French armies."

Do Englishmen ever ask themselves why the
Duke of Marlborough fought the Battle of Blen-
heim in the heart of Germany in
1704 ? It was a mighty victory, **Prussia Crucified in 1807.**
which drove the French armies,
80,000 strong, out of South Germany, where
they had been living on the plundered land for
years. Have Englishmen forgotten what Germany and especially Prussia endured through
the devastating invasions of the great Napoleon ?
They were simply crucified, and England more
than any other country gained from the sufferings
of Prussia. Professor A. F. Pollard has recently
reminded us that " the peace dictated by
Napoleon in 1807 robbed Prussia of more than

half her territories. Napoleon afterwards regretted he had not abolished Prussia altogether."

But let us advance to a later date, to practically modern times. From 1850 to 1870 the Third **An English** Napoleon was busy in again pre-**Panic of In-** paring destruction for Prussia when **vasion in 1859.** Bismarck arose and saved her. I am old enough to remember the terror that French ambition created, even in England, leading to the formation in 1859 of the Volunteer regiments, which in 1907 gave place under Lord Haldane to the Territorial Army. In the words of the *Cambridge Modern History*, vol. xi, p. 308 : " In December, 1855, Napoleon III was already dreaming of a great conflict of nationalities, in which France, by means of a struggle with Prussia, was to appropriate the left bank of the Rhine and *possibly Belgium also* " ! " Public opinion in England showed itself more and more hostile to Napoleon. Finally it led to the panic of invasion and the volunteer movement in 1859, both directly due to a belief in Napoleon's aggressive designs against England." Please keep that in mind to-day. " His boundless ambitions could not fail to destroy what was left of the good understanding with England." England had helped France in every way since 1850 and her reward was treachery and preparations to invade her.

There is absolutely no more reliable guide in foreign politics than the *Cambridge Modern History*, published in 1909, five years before the

World War, under the guidance of the great
historian, Lord Acton, and in its impartial
pages will be found the causes **The Rhine**
which forced Prussia under Bis- **Dream of**
marck to develop her military strength. **Napoleon III.**
"Napoleon," it writes, "knew quite well what
the French would expect from a Napoleon."
"The greatest glory, it was clear, was to be obtained by immediately realising the Napoleonic
idea, by tearing up the treaties of 1815, and by
restoring her natural frontiers to France," that
is, by annexing all German territory up to the
Rhine and also Belgium. This demand for the
left bank of the Rhine by France has been the
persistent cause of troubles in Europe, whether
her ruler was Louis XIV or the Great Napoleon,
Napoleon III, or Poincaré.

When Prussia and Austria were exhausted by
their fratricidal war of 1866 and the defeat of the
latter at Königgrätz, Napoleon saw
a chance of attaining the French **"Greed and**
dream. "As a matter of fact," **Ambition."**
writes the *Cambridge Modern History*, vol. xi,
p. 457, "there was every need of defence against
the greed of France. For just at the time of
the negotiations with the South Germans,
Napoleon suddenly came forward with his demand for compensation. The French Ambassador,
Benedetti, now received orders to demand the
left bank of the Rhine and Mainz." This demand
"afforded Bismarck fresh means of inspiring the
Southern Germans with a terror of France and

141

of thus attaching them the more closely to Prussia." The terror of France in England produced the volunteer movement and in Germany bound her kingdoms, differing in religion and culture, into one militant Empire. France may again force the nations of the world into a grand alliance to resist her.

Napoleon III quite appreciated that it was in Germany the opposition to his mad schemes had its main strength. He started **"À Berlin."** by caballing with the Emperor of Russia against Prussia, but without success. Nothing, however, could turn him from violence. The preparations and armaments, which culminated in the cry " à Berlin," were immediately pressed forward and ended in an unjustifiable declaration of war against Germany in the summer of 1870. Meanwhile, in order to keep the French Army in practice, and to sacrifice to the French Idol of Glory, Napoleon made a criminal incursion into Mexico. In fact there was no peace, but five wars in twenty years in Europe, till Prussia wrung the neck of the Gallic cock at Sedan and gave rest to Europe for nearly half a century.

During three centuries the whole policy of France, according to M. Bainville, the editor of the *Action Française*, " was to prevent Germany from realising her unity." And this was in a special degree the policy of Napoleon III, and caused him to declare war on Germany in 1870. Well might M. Victor Bérard, the distinguished

French writer, in describing her misery, write : " During these three centuries all the armies of Europe took this ' good ' Germany (*cette ' bonne ' Allemagne*) as a field of battle or encampment. *Tous les soudards la pillerent et mangerent à l'envi.*" Nine-tenths of these pillaging, destroying soldiers were French.

German Misery through Three Centuries.

I wonder if Englishmen and Americans have sufficiently recovered their balance and their sentiments of justice and fair play to meditate seriously on the full meaning of French military activity,

Piratically Plundered.

as revealed in the quotations in the preceding pages, from the highest historical authorities not only English but French. Germans have always been a peaceful folk, good citizens and good fathers, devoted to science and the fine arts, especially music. Even that intense soldier, Frederick the Great, like the Great Bismarck, owed his political power and prominence to the fact that France and Russia were always on the spring to rend to pieces the German Fatherland. The name of Hindenburg will go down to posterity side by side with theirs, and History will recognise that the Great War was one of defence for Germany and of aggression for France, in which Germany was piratically plundered of thousands of millions of pounds in the name of Reparations.

There have been few more misleading propaganda than the outcry regarding devastation in France and Belgium. It was wonderfully small,

except when caused by artillery fire. Millions
and millions of shells and other explosives
played havoc and levelled the
**Little Wanton
Destruction.** houses of many towns and villages,
but of wanton destruction there
was extremely little. Nothing like the deliberate
devastation of previous wars.

A summary survey of modern European history
would show that since the beginning of the seventeenth century French armies have
**France's
War Record.** twice crossed the Pyrénées to
attack Spain. Six times have they
crossed the Alps to attack Italy. Nine times have
they crossed the Danube to attack Austria. It
is hard to say how often they have crossed the
Rhine to ravage Germany.

Mr. Hugh F. Spender, one of the best informed
writers on European affairs at the present time,
stated in *The Fortnightly Review* of
**A War Budget
in 1929.** June, this year, 1929, " France is
now spending 58 million sterling on
her military budget, as compared with 34 millions
in 1925," an increase of 24 millions in four years,
whilst the total war budgets of the nations of
Europe exceed 700 millions sterling. What does
it mean ? What does it portend ?

An even more important witness to the war
madness of France is Senator William E. Borah,
the very distinguished Chairman of the Committee on Foreign Affairs at Washington, who
made in the London *Observer* of the 17th May,
1925, the following statements, and be it noted

that they were made in the year that the French war budget was only 34 millions, since increased by over 70 per cent.

" France has the most powerful army in the world. According to the latest reports, she has an active army of 629,012 men, a reserve army of 4,870,988 men, a total of 5,500,000 men. The army

An Army of 629,012 men in peace time.

of France, active and reserve, is more than twice that of the armies, active and reserve, of Great Britain, the United States, and Japan combined. French airplanes outnumber the British by three to one, the United States by four to one. France has more airplanes than the United States, Great Britain, and Japan combined. She has within 465 as many air pilots as the United States, Great Britain, and Japan combined. All this costs money, and, as it works out, the American taxpayer is not only paying the cost of our own military establishment, but is, in fact, paying for the maintenance of the French military establishment, or a large portion of it, and at a time when the French taxpayers' taxes are less than one-half of what they are in the United States."

The same fact is true of England. The British taxpayer, by paying the interest on the French loan, is, together with the American citizen, providing nearly the whole cost of the enormous French military

A Menace to England.

and naval establishments. A very large part of this establishment is a direct menace to Great

The Irish Future

Britain. France is building up a " War Reserve " of 4,800 modern aeroplanes. Its present peace strength is 1,260, of which 990 are in Europe, but very much worse from the British standpoint is the naval outlook. The *Moniteur de la Flotte*, the semi-official organ of the French Admiralty, gave full details recently. By the year 1931 she will possess the following modern vessels : 12 cruisers, 6 of them 10,000 tons each, the largest size permitted under the Washington Agreement, and armed with 8-inch guns ; 100 modern torpedo-boat destroyers, 27 of which will approximate to small cruisers and which have the abnormally high range of action of 3,000 miles. Fifty of these destroyers will be armed with 5·1-inch guns. And, last but not least, she will have 70 submarines, most of them of the large sea-going type. It must not be forgotten that Germany started the late war with less than 30 submarines, several of which were only suitable for coastal work. This is a grandiose programme. At present there are *in commission* "The largest submarine yet designed." " forty-two submarines, classified as follows : One diving cruiser of 3,000 to 3,500 tons, the largest undersea vessel yet designed ; 14 ocean submarines of 1,500 tons, with a wide radius of action ; six ocean boats of 1,100 tons ; 19 coastal boats of 600 tons ; two submarine minelayers." In case of war, could British Commerce survive for a week in the Channel and the Mediterranean ? The British Admiralty may be trusted to demand ships to counterbalance this increase of French naval power, and particularly anti-submarine craft.

The audacity of French statesmen, in refusing to pay even interest on war loans, is almost incredible, seeing that at the beginning of this year (1929) they proposed a reduction **£80,000,000 Surplus.** in taxation by twelve millions sterling, and this large amount will certainly be greatly exceeded. *The Times* of the 25th September, 1929, made the following almost incredible statement : " The revenue has already exceeded the estimates by 6,000,000,000f. (£48,000,000), and it is expected that by the end of the year the surplus will be in the neighbourhood of 10,000,000,000f. (£80,000,000). The promised relief of taxation is estimated to represent a loss to the revenue of only 6,000,000,000f. so that there is still foundation for the complaint that the burden of taxation is unnecessarily heavy." A Budget surplus of £80 millions almost passes belief. Even if £48 millions go to relieve the French taxpayer, a large part of the remaining £32 millions should go to England, which every year is paying £100 millions as interest on the loans made to the Allies.

The French should not be astonished by our anxiety in regard to their naval developments. Against whom do they need submarines by the score on their western coast ? The language of their Press is a constant irritant. The *Daily News* of London was horrified by " the orgy of anti-British caricature in the French Press and on the French stage. Everybody and everything British was held up, not to good-natured laughter, but to the bitterest hatred, ridicule, and contempt. From being allies and heroes, we were in a few months transformed into the standing targets of popular abuse ; no mud was too dirty to throw at us. This went on for over four years, and was extended far outside France itself into countries such as Belgium, wherever there were newspapers and theatres under French influence. The whole force of French propaganda seemed exerted to make Britain and the British odious." In describing the incidents of the Treaty of Versailles, Mr. Lloyd George remarked, " Let me say in passing that I felt very sorry for President Wilson in that difficult time. What shattered his nerves and broke him down completely was the scurrilous abuse to which he was continuously subjected in the French Press. I am accustomed to abuse. I have been abused throughout my public life, from the very first moment I entered it, but President Wilson had never experienced anything like it. It was to him a new and stunning experience and it broke him." It is difficult to imagine anything more odious. Only the other day Mr. Philip Snowden experienced something very similar.

CHAPTER IX

HOW GERMANY WAS FORCED INTO WAR

(i) "In a few years more the Tsar's Government would have so developed its railway system as to obtain a permanent and crushing advantage. With this consideration is very closely connected the hastening of the war." "That consideration, as we ourselves firmly believe, is what finally decided the German Emperor to make the war now instead of a couple of years hence."—

> Mr. J. L. Garvin
> in *The Observer*,
> January, 1915.

(ii) "The German army is vital, not merely to the existence of the German Empire, but to the very life and independence of the nation itself, surrounded as Germany is by other nations, each of which possesses armies about as powerful as her own. . . . Germany has nothing which approximates to a two-Power standard. She has, therefore, become alarmed by recent events and is spending huge sums of money on the expansion of military resources."—

> Mr. Lloyd George
> in January, 1914

WHAT "the recent events" referred to by Mr. Lloyd George were was made clear within six

months. On the 3rd June, 1914, exactly two
months before the war, the military correspondent
of the London *Times*, Colonel
Repington, in an article on " Europe
under Arms " explained how well
founded were German fears of Russian preparations. He pointed out that Russia had increased
her " peace establishment " (!) by 150,000, making
a total " peace strength of about 1,700,000, or
approximately double that of Germany . . . next
door to a mobilisation in times of peace." Yes.
It was a real efficient mobilisation nine weeks
before the War. It was exactly parallel with our
mobilisation of our Fleet at the Spithead Review,
two weeks before the War. " There are signs that
Russia has done with defensive strategy. The
increased number of guns, the growing efficiency
of the Army, and the improvements made or
planned in strategic railways are again matters
that cannot be left out of account. These things
are well calculated to make the Germans anxious."
Rather, and within eleven weeks Russia had
thrown 1,000,000 men and 3,000 cannon into
East Prussia. During the preceding two years
the great French armament factories at Creuzot
had supplied Russia with 6,000 field guns, the
famous 7·5's. The Russian Army was thoroughly
prepared for the Great Adventure. So was the
British Fleet. There remained only the murder
of the Austrian Archduke needed to let loose
Armageddon on the ignorant, innocent peoples
of Europe.

Col. Repington on Russian Mobilization.

The Irish Future

In General Sir C. E. Caldwell's *Life of Field-Marshal Sir Henry Wilson*—" The man who made the War," as he is frequently called —it is noted at page 107 that Lord Grey in his *Twenty-five Years* freely **Six Years' Plotting admitted.** admits that " several of his colleagues were entirely unaware that conversations between our General Staff and those of France and Belgium had been sanctioned six years before the War and had been *in progress long before* the Agadir crisis arose."

The first point, in fact, that must be remembered is that the War began in 1905 and not, some nine years later, in 1914. Before the former date, the Con- **The Salisbury Policy.** servative Government had, indeed, made serious gaps in the tried policy of Lord Salisbury, which made goodwill towards Germany, if not actual alliance with her, the sheet anchor of England's foreign relations. *The Times* of the 8th January, 1924, wrote :

" With Caprivi as German Chancellor and Lord Salisbury as Prime Minister the relations between the two countries were very amicable. The close *entente*, which had existed between England and the Triple Alliance (Germany, Austria, and Italy) since 1887, continued." " The fall of the Salisbury Cabinet and the formation of a Liberal Administration tended, *as always*, to bring about difficulties with Germany. The (German) Government was much concerned by the pro-French and pro-Russian leanings of Mr. Gladstone." Madame Olga Novikoff had taken charge of

Liberal Foreign Policy. Count Hatzfeldt, the German Ambassador in London, reported to Berlin that " Lord Salisbury has shown the same confidence and the same openness as in former days,"—an honorable contrast to the secret " conversations " of Sir Edward Grey's diplomacy.

The following four paragraphs should be learned by heart by everyone who wishes to understand the origins of the War.

(i) MR. WINSTON CHURCHILL, in his truthful book, *The World Crisis*, vol. I, p. 36, declares unreservedly that " France, after her **Enormous Preparations.** treatment in 1905, had begun a *thorough* military reorganisation. Now Russia, in 1910, made an *enormous increase in her already vast army,* and both Russia and France, smarting under similar experiences, closed their ranks, cemented their alliance, and set to work to construct with Russian labour and French money the new strategic railway systems, of which Russia's western frontier stood in need."

Please note the dates 1905 and 1910, and the adjectives " thorough," " enormous," and " vast."

(ii) GENERAL BUAT, Chief of the French Headquarters' Staff in 1920, in an authoritative report to the French War Office, showed that in the spring of 1914 the French had 910,000 men in the " active " army, with 1,325,000 in reserve. " One may say, then," he truthfully declared, " that, without taking any account of the Belgian Army (300,000 men) or the four British Divisions,

France alone was at the beginning at least equal, if not superior, to her formidable adversary." General Sir Frederick Maurice, Chief of the British Staff, gave almost precisely similar figures in these words: " In August, 1914, before the war, the French had 817,000 Frenchmen serving with the colours and 82,000 Colonial troops." Total 899,000, *practically double their army of five years before.*

(iii) MR. GERARD, the American Ambassador in Berlin, in his *My Four Years in Germany,* p. 89, wrote : " Another reason for an immediate war was the loan made by France to Russia *on condition* that additional strategic railways were to be constructed by the Russians to Poland." That was in 1912 and Germany at once began intensive preparations. Her military backwardness before that year is shown in detail at pages 39-43. " The annual conscription in France was 50 per cent. larger than in Germany." (*Nineteenth Century,* June, 1913.)

(iv) *The Temps,* of Paris, easily the leading journal of France, in the beginning of March, 1913, recorded the colossal forces Russia was accumulating, " Within a very short period," it triumphantly wrote, " Russia will have 5,000,000 soldiers in the first line, supported by 15,000 pieces of artillery. It will be possible for Russia to throw 1,000,000 of *completely* organised troops across the enemy's frontiers within a week from the opening of hostility." A year before the War this French journal openly referred to Germany as the " enemy " whose frontiers were to be invaded and, in fact, were invaded before Germany declared war.

At the end of 1905 the secret " conversations " of Sir Edward Grey with the French War Office began. Then also com-

Concealed Alliances. menced the evil policy of concealed alliances with France, Russia, and Belgium, " to which," in Lord Morley's words " Grey has step by step been drawing the Cabinet on." The first steps were naturally elaborate and urgent military preparations by the Secretary of State for War, Mr. Haldane, which went on ceaselessly for eight years. Mr. Winston Churchill in his *Four Great Chapters of the War*, wrote : " The British Army went to France according to

"Haldane's Eight-year War Plan." what may be called the Haldane plan. Everything in that Minister's *eight-year* tenure of the War Office had led up to this and had been sacrificed for this. To place an army of four or six infantry divisions, thoroughly equipped, and with their necessary cavalry, *on the left of the French line* within twelve or fourteen days of the order to mobilise, and to guard the home island meanwhile by the fourteen Territorial divisions he had organised, was the scheme upon which, aided by Field-Marshals Nicholson and French, he had concentrated all his efforts and stinted resources." " It

" Maximum War Effort." was a modest plan ; but it was a practical plan ; it was consistently pursued and laboriously and minutely studied. It represented, approximately, the *maxi-*

mum war effort that the voluntary system would
yield, applied in the most effective and daring
manner to the decisive spot. It commanded the
assent of almost all the leading generals. When
the hour struck it worked with perfect precision
and punctuality. There was nothing to argue
about, nothing to haggle over. *The French knew
exactly what they were going to get* if Great Britain
decided to come in, and exactly when and where
they were going to get it; and mobilisation
schemes, railway graphics, time-tables, bases,
depots, supply arrangements, etc., filling many
volumes, regulated and ensured a perfect and
concerted execution. A commander whose whole
life led up to this point had been chosen. *All that
remained to be done on the day was to take the decision
and give the signal.*" On the whole the British
preparation seems to have been the most thorough
in Europe—" the maximum war effort," " dar-
ingly " carried on over eight " laborious " years.
How intense must have been the determination
of the British Cabinet to " come in." " The
French knew exactly what they were going to
get."

The British people were proud and glad to see
the great military reforms of Mr. Haldane, but
even the House of Commons had no
idea of what were the secret alliances
behind it all. The Earl of Birken-
head, with boyish delight, tells us the story of
the hoodwinking of England in the following
illuminating passage in a monograph by him on

"Dangerous and Deeply Rooted."

The Irish Future

Sir Edward Grey in *The Sunday Times* of 4th June, 1924 : " I have often amused myself by speculating what his reception would have been in the mad House of Commons of 1906 if he had informed the collection of hysterical sentimentalists *who kept him in office* of his conversations, at the time when they took place, diplomatic and military, with the French nation ; and of the commitments *deeply rooted in honour*, if not in formal documents, in which he was gradually, *dangerously*, but rightly *involving* this people. The necessity, however, for such confidences, *did not*, happily for the interests of the world, *appeal to him*, and therefore for eight years everybody was satisfied. He and Lord Haldane, with the knowledge of Mr. Asquith, made preparations for the war that threatened ; their followers made perorations on behalf of the peace which preceded it."

This is a priceless picture of a trusted statesman " dangerously " and " deeply rooting " and " involving " English " honour " in a secret war alliance with France. His duty to his country and loyalty to his colleagues " who kept him in office," did not " appeal " to him. That is the deliberate judgment on Sir Edward Grey by a Lord Chancellor of England. No doubt Mr. Asquith, as Prime Minister, was even more to blame. A camarilla of three was driving England to its doom " step by step."

Mr. Winston Churchill was equally cynical and contemptuous of England's Parliament and of the electors of the United Kingdom,—the men who were to die. In his *Four Great Chapters of the War* he gloats over their deception. " While the electors in the United Kingdom in 1906 were affirming ' by the largest majority within living memory ' their devotion to the ideals of Peace, Retrenchment, and Reform, *their trusted leader*, Sir Henry Campbell-Bannerman, was principally concerned about the Algeciras Conference and had already,—always *of course* on the express understanding that the British Government was not in any way committed to war—*authorised military conversations with the French General Staff !* "

In his *World Crisis* also, Mr. Churchill laid stress on the shameless hoodwinking of the House of Commons. " Sir Henry Campbell-Bannerman was still receiving **Shameless Hoodwinking.** the resounding acclamations of Liberals, peace-lovers, anti-jingoes, and anti-militarists in every part of the country when he was summoned by Sir Edward Grey to attend to business of a very different kind." He quite revelled in the secret betrayal of the peace-lovers. The Cabinet was overwhelmed with domestic work, the Labour attacks, education, Ireland, the struggle with the Lords, the great budget and so on, a fact that gave Grey a free hand, and he used it freely to advance his anti-German passion. In his speeches there was a more than sub-acid tone towards all things German, which Mr. Haldane, with many protestations of affection for his " spiritual home," tried to disguise.

The Irish Future

Mr. W. H. Masingham, the most cultured editor and journalist connected with the Liberal Press, in discussing Grey's un-English and anti-English conspiracy with Russia to destroy the nascent liberties of Persia and to drive out her American Minister of Finance, Mr. Schuster, wrote thus :

"Simply an Anti-German."

" The revelations of Grey's work at the Foreign Office contained in the book, *Entente Diplomacy and the World,* leave no doubt whatever as to its general character. Hostile to Liberal ideas, indifferent to liberty, deaf to the call of humanity, and careless of the peace of Europe, Grey pursued the end which, alternately schooled by the bureaucrats of France and of Russia, he put before every other purpose of British policy. He found England free. He left her anchored to the Continental system, and, as it turned out, fatally committed to the Great War. Whether or not he was sincere in his last overtures for peace must for ever remain a matter of doubt. That they were doomed to failure is a thing of no doubt whatever. A statesman cannot attain peace in three weeks when for eight years he has diligently prepared for war. In a sense, indeed, he had no policy. *He was simply an anti-German.* This fixed idea he pursued with little relevance to circumstances and with less regard to the interests of his own country. He would have gone to war over Morocco. In the Persian case it was not a question of going to war, but of destroying the liberties of a nation and, incidentally, risking the safety of India, in order to preserve at all costs the bond with Russia, which three years later he was forced to redeem in blood."

This is a hard judgment but, I fear, a true one. Grey was, according to his light, honest, but his light was the deadly darkness of anti-German diplomacy, " alternately schooled by the bureaucrats of France and of Russia." " He found England free," after many years of successful Conservative administration of the Foreign Office. He left England maimed and dethroned from her old supremacy in European affairs. History can assign no other origin for the decadence of British authority than the secret caballing of Asquith and Grey with France and Russia, the two hereditary enemies of England.

Germany was not much moved by the Anglo-French Entente of 1905, which was the work of an exceptionally able Conservative Government, with Lord Lansdowne as Foreign Minister. There might **It Meant War.** be mischief in it, but Germany had great confidence in the traditions of Lord Salisbury, represented by Mr. Balfour, and even hoped that the *entente* might have a steadying influence on France. The Liberal *entente* in 1907 with Russia, was an entirely different thing. It meant war, and the camarilla knew that and armed accordingly. Bismarck and successive German Chancellors after him used every endeavour to preserve goodwill with the Tsar's Government, and they were fairly successful. But after the quasi-revolution of 1905, due to its shameful defeat by Japan, the Pan-Slavist Party, under Isvolsky, took command of Russian foreign relations and, with the aid of Del-cassé and Millerand in France, adopted an intensely anti-German attitude. The British Government knew this fact in 1907 and Asquith, Haldane, and Grey strengthened the new *entente* in every way and proceeded immediately to prepare for war. Grey's speeches in the House of Commons threw a shield over their activities, but were listened to by small houses, almost empty benches, because not one Englishman in a thousand had any idea of the Devil's Broth that was being brewed by the camarilla. As I have said above, the French and Russian Press and the kept journals in Italy and other countries,—the bribery of numerous newspapers was never so widespread,—always wrote of him as an apostle of peace and wisdom. This ceaseless flattery in time told on a man, who was naturally modest and just, and he dwindled into becoming the mere mouthpiece of the French and Russian Foreign Offices, of Delcassé and Isvolsky.

England starts Arming in 1907.

During the four years 1906-9, when the fatal policy was finally adopted by England, I rarely failed, as M.P. for a London constituency, to hear Sir Edward Grey make his many speeches on foreign affairs, and to read in non-German Continental journals fulsome praise of his great qualities. He was the idol of the subsidised Press of Paris,

The Franco-Russian Conspiracy.

Petersburg, and Milan. These speeches were thin
and wordy. Seeking chiefly to conceal facts,
they lacked the eloquence that only truth and
straightforwardness can arouse. The self-admira-
tion of Lord Curzon was almost proverbial, but,
in a more marked degree, Grey's belief in his
inborn wisdom showed itself in every movement
of his argument. He was firmly, thick-headedly,
convinced that under his guidance English
diplomacy dominated Europe, instead of being
tied up neck and crop in the Franco-Russian
conspiracy against Germany. He knew, no doubt,
that France was prepared for any adventure that
might give her her *revanche* and again subject
German Alsace-Lorraine and the Rhineland to
the French Republic. He also knew, no doubt,
that Russian policy was every year becoming
more hostile to Germany, but I felt that he did
not fully appreciate the fact that the vast Pan-
Slavist organisation, the most active force in
Europe, made war the essence of its existence.
I had very intimate information
from Russia at that time and it all **Panslavism.**
pointed to the fact that the whole
governing caste, military and mercantile, official
and hierarchic, believed with intense conviction
that Tsarism and the old regime must rouse the
nation by a great national war or be strangled by
a universal hatred. Nothing but war,—if England joined in, successful war,—could divert the
Russian people from destroying its tyrants. From
1905, when revolution made its first great assault

on the Tsar's Government, the bureaucracy started on elaborate preparations for war, meanwhile keeping the wild beast of Socialism at bay by dummy Dumas and pretended reforms. It borrowed vast sums from France on the express condition that they should be used on strategic railways and French artillery. England, under Grey's guidance, backed the tyrants and we know the result.

Not only did Germany studiously avoid all action hostile to England, but the Kaiser almost begged for an alliance. Lord Hardinge, in his " official report " to Sir Edward Grey of his long conversation with the German Emperor at Cronberg on the 11th August, 1908, makes an almost inconceivable admission of the intense desire of the Kaiser for goodwill towards England, and, if possible, her alliance :

Kaiser Pleads for Goodwill.

" Towards the close of the interview the Emperor stopped me and said in a very emphatic manner :

" ' Remember that I fully adhere to and mean every word that I uttered at the Guildhall last year. The future of the world is in the hands of the Anglo-Teuton race. England, without a powerful army, cannot stand alone in Europe, but must lean on a Continental Power, and that Power should be Germany.'

" There was no time nor opportunity to continue what might have been an interesting discussion of a somewhat ambitious policy.

" On thinking over the Emperor's words and

the general trend of his conversation, I cannot resist the conclusion that his last sentences were *the climax to which he had been gradually leading*, and that he wished to urge *once more* the greater advantage to England of friendship with Germany over the *understandings* with France and Russia, which have already shown such beneficent and practical results during the past few years."

That was in August, 1908, when Sir Edward Grey was so frequently denying to the House of Commons the existence of such " understandings." I wonder what, in that early year of the Anglo-Russo-French alliance, were " the beneficent and practical results " indicated. " Practical " they certainly were, if they refer to the " maximum war effort in the history of the British Empire " described by Mr. Churchill. The taxpayer and the merchant, the war-widow and the war-orphan, probably have other ideals of beneficence,—so, no doubt, have the Russian people. Mr. Asquith's Government may be confidently charged with having deliberately rejected German friendship and with having half-ruined the British Empire by an undoubtedly patriotic but historically ignorant and commercially idiotic policy of war. It is in this way great empires are wrecked.

A very striking confirmation of Lord Harding's " conclusion,"—that the Kaiser's supreme desire was peace,—appeared in the *Sunday Times* of the 20th May, 1928, in a letter from General W. H. Waters, **"The Gulf of Silence."** Military Attaché at Berlin in 1901. It is almost impossible to deny to this statement of facts the highest credibility. " I was present," wrote General Waters, " at the luncheon at Marlborough House when the Kaiser pressed for an alliance. The version of his speech, for publication in the *Court Circular* of the following morning, was compiled hurriedly in the evening at Windsor by various hands so as to be in time for press. It was, as the Ambassador, the late Sir Frank Lascelles who was present at luncheon, told me, a poor production. Sir Frank wished the Emperor to publish a full report of the speech, as it was such *a statesmanlike effort to ensure peace and a reduction of armaments.* William II replied that, as he was King Edward's guest at the time of its utterance, the consent of the British Government must first be obtained."

" This consent was withheld, and the Kaiser *wrote to me* that ' it would have been a deplorable want of tact on my part if I had caused the publication in German papers, as was suggested to me from different quarters. So my words were swallowed up in the gulf of silence, and the British people, to whom they appealed, never heard of them.' "

These words of the German Emperor should be made known in every Foreign Office in Europe. The refusal of the British Government to publish the speech at the time was an act of obscurantist ill-will that almost passes belief.

The camarilla, that secretly dominated English foreign policy, without the knowledge of the

The Irish Future

English people, had adopted the summary policy, *Delenda est Germania,* and worked for it ceaselessly and with untiring energy.

The signal for war was given by the Admiralty despatching the Fleet to its "war station" on the German sea coast on the 29th July, 1914, without the authority and, indeed, without the knowledge of the British Parliament, which on that day was in session at the Palace of Westminster. This advance of the British Fleet was the first overt act of war in the Great War and history must recognise the fact. " The French knew exactly what they were going to get." They had known it for years.

The First Overt Act of War.

Mr. Churchill's account of the Cabinet meetings in the week beginning Monday, the 27th July, given at pages 193-217 in his *World Crisis* is invaluable. He definitely states that " the Cabinet was overwhelmingly pacific. At least three-quarters of its members were determined not to be drawn into a European quarrel, unless Great Britain were herself attacked, which was not likely." Then he describes the dogged assault by himself and Sir Edward Grey on this resolution, including the opening up, through Mr. F. E. Smith and Sir Edward Carson, of secret, unauthorized communications with the Conservative leaders, again without the knowledge or consent of the Cabinet. " At the Cabinet of Saturday, the 1st August," he continues, " I demanded the immediate calling out of the Fleet

" Overwhelmingly Pacific."

Reserves and the completion of our naval preparations." "The Cabinet took the view that this step was not necessary for our **The Final Meeting of the Camarilla.** safety, and I did not succeed in procuring their assent." But this step was necessary to make sure of bringing England into the War. Mr. Churchill then relates how at a secret meeting of the war camarilla, Asquith, Grey, and Haldane, at 10 Downing Street, he announced to it that "I intended instantly to mobilize the Fleet *notwithstanding the Cabinet decision.* The Prime Minister said not a single word." As I walked down the steps of Downing Street with Sir Edward Grey, he said to me, "You should **The Constitution Disregarded.** know that I have just told Cambon that we shall not allow the German Fleet to come into the Channel." This crucial decision, though communicated to the French Ambassador, was reached without the knowledge of the Cabinet. The two men were deadly afraid that their long-laid plans might "gang agley." They pushed the British Empire into war without the consent of their colleagues or of Parliament. The great Fleet went forth to war in entire disregard of the British Constitution and of the wishes of the British people, "eighteen miles of warships" Mr. Churchill tells us, "running at high speed and in absolute blackness through the narrow straits" into the German Ocean. Armageddon was let loose and England dethroned from her primacy. Mrs. Asquith has described Winston Churchill's joy next day as he skipped down the

stair-case at Downing Street, after the official declaration of war by the Cabinet.

Messrs. Asquith, Grey, Haldane, and Churchill
have an excellent excuse for their action, but
not for their secrecy, indeed secretiveness. They
honestly believed that they were carrying out
England's traditional policy of the **"We Have
Always
Fought."** Balance of Power. *The Times* of
the 4th December, 1914, tells us
"*We are not concerned to deny the charge. The
balance of power is to-day, as it has been since the
days of the Tudors, the main factor of our policy.
. . . We undoubtedly supported the Entente to preserve
that balance and to prevent the hegemony of any
single Power in Europe. . . . The maintenance of
our supremacy at sea and of the balance of power
were amongst the foundations of our traditional
policy. We have always fought for the balance of
power. We are fighting for it to-day.*"
There you have the Imperialist will-o'-the-wisp.
I don't argue that it was a bad policy, but the
hegemony, the best the world has **Our Money
on the
Wrong Horse.** ever known, that was smashed,
never, I fear, to be rebuilt, was the
world-wide predominance of the British Empire.
When a nation makes it its policy to cabal against
and form alliances against every other nation
that shows signs of strength, it is also making
war an absolute certainty. The policy of Germany was the Triple Alliance of the three
Emperors of Russia, Germany, and Austria, the
famous *Drei Kaisar Bund*, the *sole* object of

which was peace, which it maintained for nearly half a century. France holds the hegemony of Europe at the present hour and, in our semi-bankruptcy, we must acquiesce in it or go back to our old and tried alliance with Germany. Once again, in Lord Salisbury's wise saying, we put our money on the wrong horse. I can imagine my critics saying that it is unpatriotic to make such statements, but I hold that it is far worse to allow the so-called Liberal Imperialists to pose as the saviours of their country, which has suffered so cruelly from the secret, unconstitutional and mischievous methods and from the short-sightedness and ignorance of Mr. Asquith's inner Cabinet. England never again can be the greatest Power in the world, except by the renewal of her ancient friendship with Germany.

In the beginning of this chapter I have quoted *The World Crisis*, by Mr. Winston Churchill, as **"France had not a Good Case."** showing how as early as 1905 France "had begun a thorough m'litary reorganisation" and how Russia in 1910 "made an enormous increase in her already vast army." Mr. Churchill justifies these warlike preparations by a rather feeble reference to their "treatment" by Germany. France had no doubt to accept a diplomatic defeat at the hands of Germany, but, as Mr. Churchill honestly admits, she was in the wrong. "Early in 1905," he wrote, "a French mission arrived in Fez. Their language and *actions* seemed to show an intention of treating Morocco as a French Protectorate, thereby ignoring the *international* obligations of the Treaty of Madrid,"—the first treaty. "The Sultan of Morocco appealed to Germany, which was enabled to advance as the champion of an international agreement, which France was violating." Why was not Sir Edward Grey the champion? "*France had not a good case*," but Sir Edward Grey and Sir H. Campbell-Bannerman contemplated war in her support.

In April, 1904, two treaties were made by the Governments of France, Spain, and England in regard to Morocco. The first assured the world, which of course included Germany, that the integrity *A Secret Treaty.* of Morocco would be maintained and the policy of the "open door" would be applied to the trade of all nations. Germany was unmoved, but in 1905 it was discovered, to the horror of the diplomatic world of Europe, that there was a second and secret treaty, which gave Morocco over to the entire dominion of France, whilst England obtained the absolute supremacy in Egypt. The trade door was also barred against other nations, including Germany, which most justly and most reasonably protested. The French Chamber of Deputies strongly condemned this worse than back-door diplomacy and the Foreign Minister, M. Delcassé, was forced by French public opinion to resign. This secret warbreeding treaty was not very creditable to either of the "high contracting powers,"—indeed, a shameful scrap of paper.

The Irish Future

As to the " treatment " of Russia by Germany, it was certainly the most monumental idiocy in history. In his solicitude for his youthful nephew, the Kaiser pledged his Imperial word that, whilst Russia was at grips with Japan in the East, the power of Germany would protect the interests of Russia in Europe. A peace-loving fool. In 1905 the German armies could have overrun Russia and France, whilst England had not begun her preparations for war. And every crack-brained Jingo in England will tell you that hell is not hot enough for the murderous Wilhelm.

A Peace-loving Fool.

As early as the 8th March, 1915, *The Times*, at that time under Lord Northcliffe's control, and, in a special degree, the organ of the British Government, anticipated Mr. Winston Churchill's frank confessions of England's great combination with France and Russia against the German Empire. Scornfully rejecting the official myth that Britain had only intervened through solicitude for Belgium, *The Times*, now that it had done its work and justified the war in the eyes of the English people, blandly declared that the Great War had never had anything to do with Belgium or the Belgians. Had there never been a Belgium, England would have joined France and Russia against Germany all the same. In the following words *The Times* avowed the real reasons in an article entitled " Why we are at War " :

The Official Myth.

" There are still, it seems, some Englishmen

170

and Englishwomen who greatly err as to the lessons
that have forced England to draw the sword. . . .
They do not reflect that our honour and our *interest*
must have compelled us to join France and Russia,
even if Germany *had scrupulously respected the
rights of her small neighbours*. . . . The German
Chancellor has insisted more than once upon this
truth. He has fancied, apparently, that he was
making an argumentative point against us by establishing it. That, like so much more, only shows
his complete misunderstanding of our attitude and
of our character. . . . Herr von Bethmann Hollweg
is quite right. Even had Germany not invaded
Belgium, honour and *interest* would have united
us with France. We had refused, it is true, to give
her or Russia any binding pledge up to the last
moment. We had, however, *led both to understand*
that, if they were unjustly attacked (! ! !) they
might rely upon our aid. *This understanding
had been the pivot of the European policy followed
by the three Powers*. . . . If England had slunk away
from her partners in the hour of danger, on the
pretext that we had not given a technical promise
to our friends, we should never have friends
again."

It is not easy to see how the "honour" of
England was involved. History will, I am inclined
to think, decide that her honour, and perhaps her
interest also, bound her rather to her three-century-
old ally and peace than to her old and, indeed,
present enemy and war. The Liberal Imperialist
camarilla decided otherwise, and England has lost

a million of her sons and ten thousand millions of her wealth, besides her trade and prestige.

It has often struck me as almost inexplicable how experienced, honourable and patriotic men, as British Statesmen generally are, could have been guilty of the utter folly of antagonizing Germany, her best friend. For centuries, whenever England was in difficulties, Germany or rather Prussia came to her aid. I am looking at this question quite coldbloodedly, absolutely free from prejudice. My feelings are, no doubt, rather kindly towards the Austrian and the South German, but they are certainly anti-Prussian. I do not forget that the first use Prince Bismarck made of his vast power, after the defeat of France in 1871, was a venomous attack on the Catholic Church in Germany by his foolish *Kulturkampf*, which, though it imprisoned many bishops, also created the great Centre Party which has dominated German politics ever since, After the collapse of Prussian Junkerdom in the. end of 1918, Catholics, Kuno, Wirth, Stegerwald, Erzberger, Marx and others directed German affairs. Prussia's treatment of Catholic Poland was modelled on the same lines as Lord Carson's attitude to Catholics in Ulster, that is, as a helot race. Prussia has no attraction for an Irish Catholic, but she was the truest ally England ever had, and the most reliable. Her enemies were England's enemies. Canada would be a great French Dominion at the present hour, and France would have been the dominant Power in India but for Prussia.

England's best Friend.

The Irish Future

The Hon. J. W. Fortescue, *The Times* military correspondent, in July 1908, before we had begun to lie about everything connected with Germany, wrote :

" The great successes and the material gains of England during the war were mainly due to this policy "—(' the whole-hearted alliance with Prussia during the Seven Years War '). " The influence of the continental pressure upon British fortunes was strongly marked. French troops and French revenue became more and more engaged each year in the continental war, and both the French Navy and the French colonies were first starved and then abandoned to their fate. When Montcalm pleaded for support to enable him to withstand the attack which eventually destroyed French predominance in Canada, he was answered in February 1759, that it was necessary for France to concentrate the whole strength of the kingdom for a decisive operation in Europe, and therefore the aid required cannot be sent. It was the same in India, where Lally, after a gallant struggle, was overwhelmed for want of support. It was the same in the West Indies and in West Africa. The absorption of France in continental wars caused her to begin the war insufficiently armed at sea and in her distant possessions, and the same cause denied her the power of recovering herself during the campaign."

There is the plain truth. England as a Colonial Power owed her greatest over-sea conquests to Prussian aid. Waterloo also would have been a

The Irish Future

Fontenoy but for Blucher's brave battalions struggling through the night to come to Wellington's assistance. *Vorwàrts, meine Kinder,* " On, on, my children " to England's help was the cry of the old Marshal, a man of seventy, as, refusing to ride his charger, he marched on foot at the head of his veterans. There has been deep ingratitude.

Even immediately before the war the average German could not believe that England was his enemy. Men like Von Tirpitz and Hindenberg sent their sons to Oxford and Eton. Vicious anti-Germans have been telling us for years that the " Boches " looked forward to the day,—*der Tag,*—when they would destroy the British Empire.

Der Tag Real Meaning. Those who read the German Press, as I did, know that *der Tag* meant the day when they would throw back the Franco-Russian assault and free Germany once and for ever from the terrible perils he knew to be hanging over her, two simultaneous invasions from west and east. They came in 1914 and, but for England's insane misreading of history, they would both have been repulsed.

CHAPTER X

GERMANY PEACEFUL AND UNPREPARED BEFORE 1912

GERMAN HUMANITY.

(i) " The artillery with its out-of-date guns and slow and ineffective methods of fire appeared so inferior that it can have no pretension to measure itself against the French on anything approaching level terms.''

"A nation, which after all gives up little more than half its able-bodied sons to the army, has become less militarist than formerly.''—

> Col. Repington, Military Correspondent, in *The Times* of 28th October, 1911.

(ii) "How great the neglect of the Germany Army has been and how insufficient its strength can be shown to any layman. The annual conscription in France is fifty per cent. larger than in Germany in proportion to population.''—

> Mr. Ellis Barker, the very eminent publicist, in *The Nineteenth Century* of June, 1913.

BOTH these writers were notoriously anti-German and wrote after repeated visits to Germany.

The Irish Future

The former witnessed the manœuvres in Prussia in 1911.

After 1871 United Germany settled herself down to the arts of peace, first reducing her army to less than pre-war strength, whilst **The Pax Germanica.** France strained every nerve to rebuild her shattered forces. It was not till 1904, after thirty-three years, a third of a century, of peaceful development, that at last the threatening military activity of France, urged on by the Revenge (*Revanche*) Party, forced Germany to raise her army to the numbers of that of France. The *Statesman's Year Book* makes this quite plain. I quote the following figures from this most thorough and reliable publication. It is impossible to challenge the accuracy of any one of them. The French Assembly passed a law in 1886 raising the French Army on a peace footing to 500,000 men. The German Army in that year numbered 427,000. Any increase was furiously opposed and prevented by the Liberals in the Reichsrat. It was not till the Reichsrat had been dissolved and re-elected that in 1893 the German Army was increased to 479,000 men, in 1899 to 495,000, and at last in 1904 to 505,000. Forthwith France increased to 545,000. No nation had to complain of German encroachments. She sought no conquests in Europe, but by the Three-Kaiser Alliance with Russia and Austria laboured to maintain the peace of the world. Her relations with Italy were of the most friendly and the decayed industrial

life of Italy found a re-birth with the aid of
German brains, industry and money. To the same
powerful aid Japan owes her present civilisation
and greatness. Till the Asquith Government em-
bedded us in a Russian Alliance, Germany longed
for and believed in the friendship of England.

The preceding paragraph is frankly pro-German,
—with limitations. The best friends of Teutonic
culture,—a very real thing,—cannot
deny that Prussian militarism had *The Panslavist Appears.*
some very hateful aspects. Most
armies manage to evolve their Black and Tan
elements. Had, however, a wiser foreign policy
in Europe generally, and especially in England,
given German reformers, who were both powerful
and honest, a chance of clipping the wings of the
War Party, the present desolation of Europe
might have been avoided. It was a real dread of
the French *Revanche* and of the Pan-Slavic ambitions of Russia that forced every man of German
blood to stake his life and everything he possessed
in support of the Kaiser,—whom few Germans
admired or respected,—as the emblem of Germanic
Nationality and Unity. Precisely a similar state
of things, though on a very much smaller scale,
presented itself in South Africa a quarter of a
century ago. President Kruger did not represent
the mass of the Boer people. The vast majority
of the young Boers had no affection for the dopper
and his dour ways, but the continuous intrigues
and threats of Rhodes, Milner, Jameson and the gold
magnates forced the pro-English majority, including

Botha and Smuts, to stand by their wrong-headed Government in all things. Mr. Chamberlain's claim to " suzerainty " in 1897 was an assault on Boer independence and roused an intense patriotism.

I have shown in the " Pax Germanica " paragraph above that the German Army was actually smaller than that of France alone from 1871 to 1905, but it is urged by the anti-German maniacs that it was so wonderfully trained and drilled and armed that it could trample on and march over all the other armies of the world combined ! There never was such a monstrous engine of destruction. All the reliable evidence points to the fact that this masterpiece of military genius was in 1911 " old-fashioned," " antiquated " and especially " out of date " in the all-important weapons of artillery. As late as 1912 she was very unprepared for war. Colonel Repington, after witnessing the German manœuvres, wrote in *The Times*, of which he was military correspondent, on the 28th October, 1911 : " The infantry lacked dash, displayed no knowledge of the use of ground, entrenched themselves badly, were extremely slow in their movements," etc., and " seemed totally unaware of the effect of modern fire." " The cavalry was in many ways exceedingly old-fashioned ! " " The artillery, with its out-of-date material (guns) and slow and ineffective methods of fire, appeared so inferior that it can have *no pretension* to measure itself against the French on anything approaching level terms ! " And here comes the

The German Army "Old-fashioned" in 1911.

178

supreme refutation of the monstrous lies in regard
to German militarism : " A nation which after
all gives up little more than half its able-bodied
sons to the army *has become less militarist than
formerly* " ! And this is the fiendish race that
Mr. Page, the American Ambassador, assured
President Wilson had been preparing for the great
war " for forty-five years." The abyssmal ignorance of both was equalled only by the sublime
stupidity of high-minded and highly educated Englishmen, who seemed to preen themselves on their
unparalleled want of knowledge in foreign affairs.

As late as June, 1914, Mr. Ellis Barker, an eminent and extremely anti-German writer, in the
Nineteenth Century, declared : " *How great the
neglect of the German Army has been and how insufficient its strength* can be shown to any layman."
He proved that the annual conscription in France
was " *50 per cent. larger* " than in
Germany, in proportion to popula-   **" Antiquated
Tactics."**
tion. That is to say, three French
recruits were called to the colours for every two
Germans. The French Army was actually larger
in the year before the war than that of Germany,
as the French General Buat has since proved.
" The German material (chiefly cannon), also, is
scarcely up to date," continues Mr. Ellis Barker.
" The military outfit of France is superior, according to Lieutenant-Colonel Bézel of the French
Artillery and many other experts. The German
artillery is inferior to the French. The tactics of
the German Army have become antiquated."

The Irish Future

Marshal Count von Waldersee relates in his *Memoirs* that as early as 1891 " Sir Charles Dilke maintains that the progress made by the French is so enormous that we can no longer claim to be the greatest military power." Dilke had just attended the French manœuvres as Under-Secretary for War. Soon after his return I met Sir Charles in the House of Commons and nothing could be stronger than his appreciation of the French superiority, without counting the vast preparations of Russia. A memorandum, drawn up by Marshal von Moltke in 1912, denouncing the German civil authorities and the German Parliament for their gross neglect of German military requirements, has recently come to light. The German people up to 1912 resented all militarism and were entirely satisfied with their vast trade, without any warlike adventures and waste of riches and substance.

How different were the facts in England during the six years before 1912. In the first years of the war Mr. Churchill was prominent amongst propagandists in describing "that tiger spring" of Germany, as the then Attorney-General described it, on the unprepared and unsuspecting War Office innocents of Paris, Petersburg, and London. In the middle of 1916 he changed his The "Tiger Spring" of which Country? tune. His bursting vanity and very pardonable pride could not longer conceal from the world the deeds —I am glad to say the very patriotic deeds—of the Master Workmen, Haldane and Churchill. He

The Irish Future

wrote : " Certainly Great Britain's entry into the war was workmanlike. Her large Fleet disappeared into the mist at one end of the island, her small Army hurried out of the country at the other. . . . It may well be that history furnishes no more remarkable example of the determined adhesion by a Civil Government to the sound principles of war as embodied in carefully considered plans, without regard to the obvious risks and objections." It should console the average Englishman, alarmed by the myth of unpreparedness, to know that, on the contrary, Great Britain's entry into the war had been so workmanlike, and that both the naval and military activities of the British Government had in 1914, in the accurate words of the First Lord of the Admiralty, " been carefully conceived *in time of peace* and both were in harmony with the highest strategic truth." The conception had been going on for nearly nine years and naturally gave birth to vigorous offspring.

There is still intense bitterness against Germany in many an English home. Men and women do not readily forgive the slayers of their sons and husbands. The accounts of the semi-starvation of **Demented Mothers.** prisoners in German camps has added fuel to the fire of hatred. These accounts are very largely true, but they apply chiefly to the latter half of the war. It is not too much to ask English men and women to give some consideration to the fact that at this period the German people were

themselves starving. When the German Admiral
Meurer surrendered his fleet at Scapa Flow in
November, 1918, he assigned, as the chief cause
of the collapse of his country, the "appalling
mortality amongst children" and the hardly less
numerous deaths amongst the aged. One of the
first Englishmen to enter Berlin after the Armis-
tice, a bitter anti-German, told me himself of the
pitiable condition of the working-class men and
women, the vast majority of the population. He
spoke of the wan, parchment-like faces of all and
tottering steps of most. Many American jour-
nalists also recorded these facts. There were mad
demands from demented mothers for the slaughter
of British prisoners. Germany had to feed or
half-feed two millions of prisoners, and the most
hated of these unhappy men were the British,
for the German populace argued that it was their
nation that, by the naval blockade, was the
whole cause of the shortage of food. Blockade
has been said to be the most cruel of atrocities.

At the beginning of the war the feeling towards
the British was very different. *Litera scripta
manet.* There was a large English
"Sincerest Thanks." colony at Frankfort, and, before
leaving on the declaration of war, it
sent a letter to the *Frankfurter Zeitung* to say that
"as we are about to leave Germany we beg to
express our sincerest thanks to the railway, military, and police officials for the great politeness
and prevision, with which they have provided for
our journey. In expressing our heartfelt thanks

we wish to assure all Germans that, on our part, we shall do our utmost for any Germans, with whom we may be brought in contact in England!" There was no contact, as they were behind wire fences.

The Church of England chaplains of Baden-Baden and Freiburg bore the following testimony "The authorities have exhorted the inhabitants to treat foreigners with **Three Chaplains.** respect and courtesy and the people have responded nobly to the appeal. Not only have the hotel and pension keepers done everything in their power to accommodate their visitors at the most reduced prices, giving credit in many instances, but several cases have come to our notice, in which Germans have nursed and fed English women and children, who were perfect strangers to them, out of pure humanity and good feeling." The chaplain at Berlin writes in August, 1914 : " We desire further to affirm that the general attitude towards British subjects *here* has differed very little in friendliness and politeness from their attitude in times of peace." Now, were these reverend clergymen Christian gentlemen or pro-German liars ?

These statements were confirmed by many deported Englishmen. A letter in *The Times* of the 23rd September, from the spokesman of a party of 190, who **English Gratitude.** reached England through Holland, declared that " we have received kindness everywhere " in Germany. One of a party from Dantzic tells us that " The Germans have been absolutely stunning to us ! " " We had no lack of money. The Germans were constantly asking us whether we wanted any." English cheques were freely cashed. May I relate a personal episode ? My brother, an aged invalid, since deceased, was at this time at the Sanatorium of St. Blasien in the Black Forest and returned to London. His German doctor accepted a cheque of £10 for his fees and the hotel at which he was staying another cheque of that amount for his last week's account. The manager also gladly cashed a cheque for £10 to meet his railway expenses, and just as my brother was driving off to the station he ran after the carriage to press on the invalid another £10, as he feared that the first might be insufficient for a long journey. These four cheques of £10 each have been con-fiscated by the British Government under a shameful provision of the Treaty of Versailles and two kindly Germans have been mercilessly mulcted. As my brother's executor, I had my-self to pay up, out of his estate, to His Majesty's Treasury the £40 due to them !

The question of the British prisoners' camps has not been fairly dealt with. There was much hardship during the middle and end of the war, but even after a year of warfare the Very Rev. Herbert Bury, Church of England Bishop of North and Central Europe, was able to write to *The Times* of the 4th September, 1915, a letter in which he declared that " our chaplain in Berlin, the Rev.

An English Bishop and an American Ambassador.

The Irish Future

H. M. Williams, assures me that in the camps where he has been allowed to go in the way of visiting and ministering, the authorities were ever courteous and helpful and, in his judgment, doing their best to mitigate the hardships of imprisonment for the men." He added, " That is what I hear from other correspondents also, and we have great reason to be grateful to the commandants of the different camps in Germany and in many instances to their wives also." On the 1st September, 1915, the *Morning Post* published the following statement : " The American Ambassador at Berlin sent to the British Foreign Office two reports by an official of the Embassy, Mr. Jackson, who had visited camps for prisoners of war." One report, on the camp in Westphalia, stated that " it is beautifully situated in a healthy place and is arranged for 10,000 prisoners, housed in barracks which accommodate 500 men each, all being provided with stoves. With all the British prisoners I talked freely, out of hearing of any German, and none had any important complaint to make. The food which I tasted was good. The French cooks told me that the material furnished is good and I saw that the kitchens were clean and well arranged. Meat is provided three times a week. The canteens seemed well stocked and the baths well arranged." I could give other evidence of good treatment before the deadly grip of the British naval blockade brought starvation to all, but none as authoritative as the above from a bishop and an ambassador.

CHAPTER XI

THE GERMAN FLEET AND TRADE RIVALRY

THE UNITED STATES IN SOUTH AMERICA

(i) "Britain began this war fully prepared and as if she expected it. Germany was thoroughly unprepared and undoubtedly did not expect war with England."—

> Mr. A. H. Pollen, at the Mansion House,
> April, 1915.

(ii) "At the time (June 1914) of the Kiel regatta there was not any intention of going to war on the part of Germany."—

> Mr. Winston Churchill,
> December, 1923.

(iii) "Lord Haldane said to me, 'I do not believe that the German Emperor and his advisers really wanted war '."—

> Very Rev. Dean Inge,
> January, 1929.

(iv) "July 28th—A note came from Asquith (Secretary of State for War) ordering the 'Precautionary Period' (Semi-mobilisation). This we did. I don't know why we are doing it, *because there is nothing moving in Germany.* We shall see. The Russians have ordered the mobilisation of 16 Corps."

186

The Irish Future

"July 30th—Nicholson (Under Secretary, Foreign Office) expects German mobilisation to-morrow."

"July 31st—Eyre Crowe told me that Germany had given Russia 12 hours to demobilise. Russia's answer was an order for 'General Mobilisation'."

> Diaries of Field Marshal Sir Henry Wilson,
> Director of Military Operations,
> page 153.

How many Englishmen of the present day are aware that it was possible in the second year of the war to make the first of the above statements, yet it was made on the 30th April, 1915, ten months **England "Thoroughly Prepared."** after war began, at the Mansion House in the heart of London, in a lecture by a gentleman, who had long been recognised as a prominent naval authority and expert. It is emphasised by the even more important declaration by Mr. Churchill, a declaration made on oath.

The question arises immediately: Was the anti-German agitation by the Asquith Government in 1908-10 in regard to battle-ships an honest criticism or an **"Goading their Followers."** extremely unscrupulous political manœuvre? *The Times* of the 23rd October, 1924, ten years after the War began, at last told the truth and the whole truth. It admitted that the building of dreadnoughts started the whole naval competition, adding: "Nobody, however, cared to acknowledge it, and the responsibility

for the consequent increase in the British Fleet
was ascribed solely to the German armaments.
In reality, however, Germany *was building no
faster* than the rate laid down in the Naval Law
of 1900. The Liberal Cabinet of Mr. Asquith
and Sir Edward Grey painted the German danger
in the blackest colours, in order *to goad their unwilling followers* to increased sacrifices. It was
the year of the Navy Scare, the fleet panic.
British newspapers, theatres, cinemas scared the
' man in the street ' with the bogy of a German
invasion. Sir Edward Grey and other leading
politicians overwhelmed the German Ambassador
with requests that he should urge the reduction
of German naval armaments. Count Wolff-
Metternich, a weak man, on his part did not cease
to bombard the Kaiser and Chancellor with
pessimistic reports." The Navy Scare was thus,
according to *The Times*, a put-up job, intended to
mislead the British people, an utterly unscrupulous
manœuvre. " Goading their unwilling followers "
by " painting the German danger in the blackest
colours " is a very moderate description of those
evil days in the House of Commons. I remember
them well. How can the British Foreign Office
expect ever again to be believed by the statesmen of
Europe ? The expression " *Perfide Albion* " will
have another run of life.

I beg to reproduce on the opposite page two
diagrams published in the *Statesman's Year Book*
for 1908, the most reliable, able, and authoritative
volume of political statistics in the world. These

Diagram I

TOTAL NUMBER OF SHIPS IN VARIOUS NAVIES CARRYING GUNS EQUAL OR SUPERIOR TO THOSE OF "DREADNOUGHT" (12 INCH, 45 CAL.)

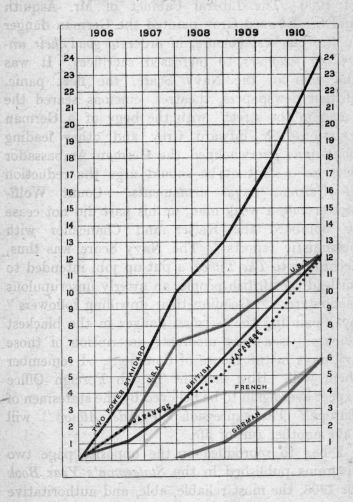

N.B.—In 1907 France had three Dreadnoughts before Germany had one. Diagram II is still more convincing.

Diagram II

TOTAL NUMBER OF SHIPS IN VARIOUS NAVIES CARRYING GUNS EQUAL OR SUPERIOR TO THOSE OF THE "KING EDWARD" CLASS (12 INCH, 40 CALIBRE)

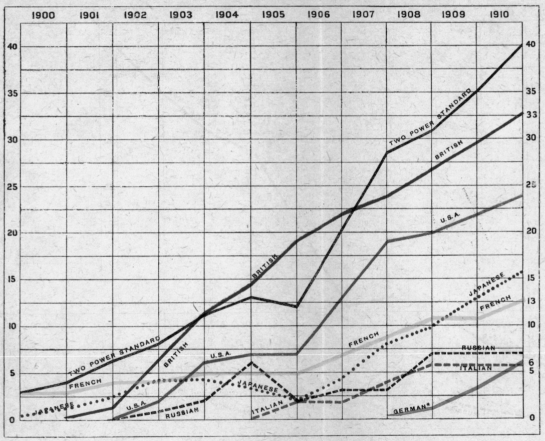

N.B.—In 1910 Germany had the smallest navy of any of the Great Powers.

diagrams in the first and last columns present for the great Naval Powers not only the number of ships in existence in 1908, but those projected up to 1910. The red and green lines in both diagrams show the impassable superiority of the British Navy over that of Germany in battleships of the first and second classes, known in England as Dreadnoughts and King Edwards. So enormous was this superiority that it is apparent to the most casual observer. Not only was there an unapproachable superiority in numbers but, as Mr. Churchill tells in his *World Crisis*, p. 122, " no fewer than twelve ships were actually building on the slips for the Royal Navy, armed with these splendid weapons," the new 13·5 guns, throwing a shell of 1,400 lbs., " quite unsurpassed in the world and firing a projectile nearly half as heavy again as the biggest fired by the German fleet," which was a 1,000-lb. shell. Turning to France, the yellow line made clear that, in 1908, she had four Dreadnoughts to one of Germany, and in 1910 would have six to six. In second-class but still very powerful battleships France in 1910 would have thirteen, Russia seven and Germany six. Was not Germany justified in having a naval programme to protect the trade of Dantzic and Memel in the Baltic against Russia and to safeguard against France the far greater commerce of Hamburg and Bremen, facing the Atlantic ?

Mr. Asquith's camarilla knew, though many

189

members of his Cabinet seemed not to know, that at that time the alliances with France and **Four-fold Strength of Allies.** Russia—alliances is the only truthful word—placed at the disposal of the Allies a battleship strength four times that of Germany. History must come to the conclusion that this agitation was due not to any fear for the fleet of England but for the fleets of France and Russia. If Germany could be frightened into stopping the building of battleships, the two latter Powers would have a great predominance over those of Germany and could destroy her commerce and blockade her coasts. Again and again I protest that I attribute nothing of bad faith to the British people or to the British Parliament, of which I was then a member, but I do allege that there is strong evidence that down to the last pre-war day the British people and the British Parliament were hoodwinked, misinformed, and misled by Mr. Asquith.

What extreme justification there was for the German refusal to stop battleship building was **A Very Big Programme.** brought to light *after the War* by the publication by the Revolutionary Government at Petrograd of many secret political papers. One of these was a detailed report, dated the 2nd February, 1911, in which M. Isvolski, the Russian Ambassador in Paris, informed his Chief, M. Sasanoff, the Russian Foreign Minister at Petersburg, that the French Government had adopted a new programme for the French navy, in which provision was made

for sixteen new battleships, six new cruisers,
twenty destroyers, and fifty submarines! This
very, very big programme was actually much
larger than the German one of the same period,
but it met with no hostile criticism from Mr.
Asquith's Admiralty Chiefs or from Sir Edward
Grey. How they lied in the House of Commons!

Far and away the most important revelation
came, also after the War, from Grand Admiral
von Tirpitz, who, in his book,
Political Documents, records that **"France lays down big Ships."**
when Mr. Haldane, the British War
Minister, had his historic conversation with the
Kaiser in the Schloss at Berlin, on the 9th February, 1912, "H.M. the Kaiser pointed out that
in view of the extended programmes of *our Continental neighbours alone*, we had already been
compelled to keep the development of our fleet
up to standard. To this Haldane made certain
observations to the effect that Great Britain
would take care that the French and Russian naval
programme would not increase too rapidly. But
he refused to go further into *any concrete question*
as to the position with regard to France in this
matter, since France was laying down three big
ships in 1912, while we were considering whether
ultimately we would build only two ships."

Von Tirpitz alleges that the Haldane proposals,
which would probably have led to a peaceful
compromise, were wrecked by M. Poincaré, the
French President, who refused to accept any
limitation of her Navy on the part of France.

The Irish Future

The day will certainly come when all just men must hold the German people guiltless of any thought of aggressive war. They were forced, as Mr. Lloyd George said on the 1st January, 1914, to struggle for " the very life and independence of the German nation itself."

The Times of the 23rd October, 1924, commenting on these revelations, remarked : " It is **Revelations of Admiral von Tirpitz.** *something of a surprise* to find that in the period of 1905-1906 Admiral Tirpitz was against the scheme for increasing the German Fleet, and opposed it with all his power in the interest of maintaining peace with Great Britain. The documents show that in the first phase of the struggle a state of extreme tension arose between the Kaiser and the Chancellor, Prince von Bulow, on the one side, and Admiral von Tirpitz on the other."

In the end, Admiral von Tirpitz proved victorious, though only after sending in his resignation to the Kaiser. He depicts a **Von Tirpitz resigns.** lively scene, which took place in the Palace in Berlin when the Kaiser realised that he declined to co-operate in accelerating the shipbuilding programme and the slow rate of building, laid down by the Naval Law of 1900, was maintained.

Not only was the Grand Admiral opposed to any action which might irritate England, **Von Moltke opposes war.** land, but the military chiefs took the same line. *The Times* records that General von Moltke, Chief of the Army Staff, declared that, in his view, war with England must be avoided, and all this time the Liberal Government and its newspapers were working up an intense hatred of Germany for its desire and preparations to destroy the British Navy and the British Empire.

The most honourable comment on the naval agitation by Mr. Asquith also appeared in the columns of *The Times,* when its Paris correspondent, Sir Thomas Barclay, asked very pertinently : **Honourable Comment by *The Times.*** " Will the French Navy be free to increase indefinitely while the German Navy is in agreement with us not to do so ? . . . It has obviously become *imperative* for Germany to increase her fleet in proportion to the needs of its protection against an efficient French fleet." Germany has been much blamed for not accepting the " naval holiday " suggested by Mr. Churchill, but both France and Russia refused to be bound by it. Why was that fact concealed from the British Parliament ? Germany was oppressed with terror at the idea of her great trade being destroyed and Hamburg and the Kiel Canal blockaded by a French fleet. It was a far greater danger than any that England could possibly be exposed to.

There cannot be a shadow of a doubt that what chiefly moved English sentiment against Germany was commercial rivalry. The great anti-free-trade organ, the **Commercial Rivalry.** *Morning Post*, on the 25th May, 1916, let the cat out of the bag in this passage :

"Before the War this country was sinking into the position of industrial and commercial dependence upon Germany. In the cloth trade we were falling into the position of supplying Germany with yarns and wool, which she worked up into cloth ; in the steel trade, the chief source of strength in war, Germany was producing double the output of the United Kingdom. In the smelting of other metals Germany was supreme ; in glass and silk we had gone almost out of business; in sugar, which, like cloth, had once been almost a British monopoly, we depended upon Germany. In the electrical trades we maintained a precarious and secondary position. Even upon those industries, in which we seemed to maintain our lead, Germany had a strong hold. Thus our textiles lay at the mercy of German dyes; our confectionery of German sugar ; our ship-building relied upon German steel shafting. And in our commerce Germany had as strong a position as in our industry. In banking and on the wool, cotton, leather and stock exchanges the German influence was growing, if not supreme."

British trade "Sinking before the War!" There never was more blatant commercial idiocy or more wilful lying. Before the **Booming British Trade.** War British trade was bounding and bursting in its prosperity, chiefly on account of the development of our trade with Germany and the United States. In fifteen years, just the very period of German competition, imports and exports practically doubled from £764,558,690 in 1898 to £1,404,151,093 in 1913 (*Statesman's Year Book*). This increase was real, every penny, and in no way influenced by the value of sterling exchange, as might be the case at the present time.

Lord Rothermere, in the *Sunday Pictorial* of a date so late as the 25th November, 1923, stated : " For the last twenty-five years before the War British trade was carried along not by its own momentum but rather by the rapidly increasing prosperity of the world in general." This dictum means, if it means anything, that, so far as Europe was concerned, British trade advanced by the aid of German trade.

The all-important point, however, is that of all the countries of the world Germany was the only one that bought from England **Germany our** nearly as much as she sold to us. **only Big** In the words of Mr. Harold Cox, the **Buyer.** distinguished economist, " Indeed, next to India, Germany was absolutely the best of our pre-War customers." Whilst the United States sent us goods to the value of £141,704,000 in 1913, they bought only £29,297,000. France sold us £46,349,000 and took only £28,957,000 of British goods. Russia sold us £40,275,000 and bought only £18,116,000 of our manufactures. On the other hand our best customer, Germany, sold us £80,551,000, *but bought* £60,573,000 *worth of the produce of the British Empire.* In 1906 the figures had been £38,000,000 and £34,000,000, respectively. By destroying German commerce we cut our own throats. Little wonder that the working men of

England, the Labour Party, regard the so-called governing classes of the past, especially the Liberals, as their most stupid advisers.

It is a known fact that very few persons read statistics and still fewer try to understand them, —least of all that purblind and **A most vicious attack.** wholly unreliable body, the British Foreign Office. There have not been many more elaborate notes on European politics for a century than the late Sir Eyre Crowe's secret memorandum of January, 1907, on our relations with Germany, and it does not devote a line to our trade with her. So wanting in impartiality was this document that Lord Sanderson, who had been Under-Secretary at the Foreign Office during Lord Salisbury's administration, took the extreme course after his retirement of criticising its misstatements and its anti-German spirit. Sir Eyre Crowe's memorandum was, in fact, an amazingly inaccurate and most vicious attack on German policy, suppressing every fact unfavourable to the policy, which the Foreign Office knew had already been fixed on by the Liberal Imperialist Camarilla. A couple of Lord Sanderson's remarks deserve quotation. They refer to " eventual trade developments in Morocco and China."

" M. Delcassé," he wrote, " ignored Germany entirely when he commenced operations in Morocco." "But in addition there is **Isolating Germany.** no doubt that M. Delcassé was steadily pursuing a series of manœuvres for the purpose of isolating Germany and weakening her alliances." The French attack was directed not only against German trade, but against her political position. Lord Sanderson incidentally referred to the German policy in regard to the Boer War. " Their conduct towards us, though not particularly gracious, was perfectly correct. I see no reason to doubt that Germany declined Mouravieff's invitation to join a European League for the purpose of offering and pressing mediation " in favour of the Boers. The secret despatches published by the Soviet Government since the War prove the loyalty of Germany in this French manœuvre. " The German Emperor altogether refused any encouragement to President Kruger when he came over to Europe " though he received an ovation from the French Government. During the Boer War " the protests of Germany against our method of exercising the right of search were, no doubt, rude but not altogether without excuse. The almost simultaneous seizure of *three large German mailships*, laden with passengers and cargo, two of which were searched from top to bottom without finding the smallest evidence to justify the **Seizure of German ships. "Intolerable."** step, and the third of which was, no doubt, equally innocent, was an act, which, *if practised on ourselves* would have certainly been denounced as *intolerable*." These acts were in the opinion of all nations outrages on a friendly power. Can anyone wonder that the United States have definitely said that they will never again put up with such treatment ?

The Irish Future

Probably the most dangerous act of the British Foreign Office, one which would have ousted

Ousting the German from China. German trade from the richest part of China, is described by Lord Sanderson in these words :

" We had in February, 1898, obtained from the Chinese Government a public engagement that no territory should be alienated in the provinces adjoining the Yangtse and the language of the English Press indicated a tendency to regard the valley of that river as the proper sphere of English influence in any partition of interests. The Germans were keen to prevent our acquiring exclusive rights or privileges in this enormous and important tract of country,"—the finest trade area in the Chinese Empire. " The German Emperor told Sir F. Lascelles (our ambassador at Berlin) that he was ready to give us his general support in China, provided we would engage to observe the policy of the open door in the Yangtse Valley. *At that time our relations with Germany were decidedly friendly.*" An agreement was arrived at in October, 1900, which placed on record a community of policy " which the German Government valued, no doubt, mainly on the ground that it kept the Yangtse open to German industrial enterprise." Lord Sanderson added, " I have written these notes because they tend to show that the history of German policy to this country is not the unchequered record of black deeds which the Memorandum (of Sir Eyre Crowe) seems to portray." Indeed, he makes it quite plain that the boot was on the other foot, and that it was France and England which sedulously worked to hamper German commercial activity in world trade. The Continental League formed by Mr. Asquith's Government against Germany and the consequent war were almost entirely due to the clashing of commercial interests.

At the present time it is increasingly manifest that the markets of the South American republics are the object of very far-reaching designs, both in England and the United States. Germany, before the Great War, also had widespread commercial connections, which disappeared completely from the first day of the world conflict. British interests also were wounded almost unto death. America, very naturally, took advantage of the position and developed her business in every field of southern trade, of which she secured practically a monopoly. In 1912 United States investments in the ten largest South American countries were estimated, according to an article in the *Edinburgh Review* of April, 1929, at 174,000,000 dollars, which in last year, 1928, had increased a dozenfold to 2,167,000,000 dollars. After the war almost the first effort of Great Britain was to recover and, if possible, improve her old position. Her most striking manifestation was the visit of the Prince of Wales in 1925 to the southern capitals, and his outspoken call to British commerce. The rival aspirant to trade hegemony soon appeared in the person of Mr.

Rivalries in South America.

Hoover, who travelled over the same road as soon as his Presidency of the U.S.A. had been assured. England was not slow to counter this exceptional move by the appointment of a special committee of experts, under the chairmanship of Lord D'Abernon, to study South American trade in the republics. It has been singularly successful, having secured £8,000,000 worth of contracts in a couple of weeks. In fact, the race is becoming fast and furious in a manner that cannot fail to get on the nerves of the great commercial and financial combinations involved on both continents. In the past the theory of Admiralty most in favour has been the need of showing the flag on every ocean, because, it is nakedly declared, trade follows the flag. That the British sea-lords firmly believe in this well-founded theory is proved by the whole naval history of England, and it is quite certain that the admirals at Washington have learned the same lesson very thoroughly and with a dangerous rivalry.

In the middle of 1921 we were very near a squabble with the United States about the trade and mines of the Canton Province. Professor Dewey, the distinguished American writer, described in the *New Republic*, of the 6th July of that year, the very important concessions obtained by a British consortium to the detriment of American interests. " This coal concession is one of the most remarkable in all the history of predatory imperialistic finance. It conveys to the British syndicate the right to work the coal of the province, and, after enumerating 22 districts, even, adds to the long list an elastic ' etc.' Further it binds the provincial government to help in expropriating the owners of any prior unworked concession for coal mines. To this monopoly of coal is added what is practically a monopoly of transport, for with it goes the right to construct any roads, railways, or waterways in the province."

It is to be feared that the commercial exploiter may be in the future, as in the past, the parent of internecine feuds in more than one continent. We must forge a chain to shackle his ubiquitous meddling.

CHAPTER XII

ATROCITIES—LOUVAIN AND RHEIMS— THE SUBMARINES AND ADMIRAL SIMS

WHAT IS TRUTH?

" The French burnt every town and hamlet through
which they passed, murdering the peasants and outraging
the women, totally destroying the magnificent convent of
Alcobaca, the Bishop's Palace at Leiria, and many other
fine buildings, with the mere object of vengeance on the
country, to which they had come as professed friends."—

Sir Herbert Maxwell's *Life of Wellington*,
describing the French retreat from
the lines of Torres Vedras.

UNDER the attractive heading of " Lying as a
Fine Art " a recent writer in *The Times* reminds
us that : " The Turcomans have a
"Systematic Poisoning." folk-tale concerning a youth, who
escaped execution and won the
Khan's daughter as a bride by telling, one after
another, forty incredible lies." I wonder what
would be a becoming reward for the propagandists
of Crewe House. A harem, at least. A few
months ago Mr. Rudyard Kipling informed the

202

students of a Scottish University that to lie was
the first use the first man made of the gift of
speech, and who, after the past ten years, will
deny the accuracy of this very Christian gentleman ? I fear he was thinking of his own language
at Southampton in June, 1915, when he assured
his audience that : " If Germany is victorious
every refinement of outrage which is within the
compass of the German imagination will be inflicted on us in every aspect of our lives." " The
alternative for us is robbery, rape of women,
starvation as a prelude to slavery. That is the
truth." Dean Inge, of St. Paul's Cathedral, was
still more maniacal as late as the 30th November,
1922, when in the *Evening Standard* he described :

" *In truth* the temper in which Germany began
the War. The Germans meant to conquer the
world, and in doing so to perpetrate massacres
of non-combatants on a scale, which would throw
the exploits of Attila, Genghiz Khan and Timour
into the shade. The Kaiser and his Ministers
would have been quite unable to keep down the
demon, which their systematic poisoning of the
public mind had raised."

" Systematic poisoning of the public mind,"
also called " truth," is delightful. I have heard
similar truth preached from the altar of the Prince
of Peace by the late Father Bernard Vaughan,
whilst the Rev. J. A. Mulry, the President of
the Fordham Catholic University in New York,
told a congregation of pious Irish that when the

The Irish Future

U.S. Government proclaimed war "it was as though God Himself stood in my presence and said ' I call you to war.' "

These and other reverend gentlemen may take to heart four simple facts :

(*i*) The first act of the new French administration of Alsace-Lorraine was to evict the Crucifix of Christ from the public schools, where the Germans held it in honour.

(*ii*) The French military authorities, in invading German territory, have forced the Municipal authorities of the Catholic Rhineland,—the best Catholics in the world, "the most docile, the most hard working and the most intelligent people in Europe," as General Smuts described them,—to provide brothels for their Negro African troops. Mr. Norman Angel has described this abomination in the *Contemporary Review* of September, 1926.

(*iii*) When some twenty years ago the infidel Government of France confiscated all Catholic Churches and buildings, the Paris *Figaro* reported that the communist municipality of Vendôme had gone one better by converting a Catholic Church and its grave-yard into a public latrine.

(*iv*) Cardinal Logue, the Archbishop of Armagh, stated in October, 1914, that : "He did not believe there was any use in having Catholic chaplains in hospitals in France. He saw a formula to be signed by any soldier before he could have a priest in these hospitals. This formula and the requirements of this condition were devised from the beginning to deprive dying

The Irish Future

Catholic soldiers of any chance of receiving the Sacraments."

I speak with feeling as a Catholic and an Irishman. He knows little of the history of the sixteenth century who is unaware that the success of the Reformation was chiefly due to a shameless propaganda that represented every priest and nun as at best disreputable. The chapters in Dean Maitland's *Dark Ages*, entitled "The Ribalds," give a few examples of the unclean charges made. As a young man I travelled much in Europe, and everywhere came up against the lies and scurrilities of the enemies of Ireland.

"The Ribalds."

I will now attempt to appreciate a few of the charges laid against the German armies and people in the early days of the War. The blood-curdling report of the British Commission, under the chairmanship of Lord Bryce, refers entirely to this short period. During this time the German military authorities were particularly anxious to conciliate American opinion, and the correspondents of American journals were allowed to move about the war area with extraordinary freedom. After about two months of war four American correspondents, Mr. Roger Lewis, of the Associated Press ; Mr. Irvin S. Cobb, of the *New York Evening Post* ; Mr. Henry Hanson, of the *Chicago Daily News* ; and Mr. James Bennett, of the *Chicago Tribune*, horrified at the monstrous charges made, issued a joint memorandum,—it is too long to quote in

"Professional and Personal Word and Honour."

full,—in which they pledged their "professional"
and "personal" word and honour that after
many weeks with the German Army in Belgium
they had not seen "a single instance" of atrocity.
"So far as we have seen there has been no mis-
treatment of civilians by soldiers." Mr. Irvin
Cobb subsequently added : "Every one of the
refugees had a tale to tell of German atrocities
on non-combatants, but *not once* did we find an
avowed eye-witness to such things. Always our
informant had heard of the torturing or maiming
or the murdering, but never had he personally
seen it. It had always happened in another
town." "Though sundry hundreds of thousands of German soldiers had gone this way no
burnt houses marked their wake." These American gentlemen may have been modern Ananiases,
but there is nothing *a priori* to suggest that they
were liars. Even the special correspondent of
the *Daily Mail*, writing from Rouen in the first
week of September, 1914, stated : "Certainly
panic in Normandy seems wholly unwarranted.
I feel bound to mention the report of M. Goubet,
Councillor-General of the Pas de Calais, who
arrived here last night, in regard to alleged Uhlan
atrocities in the north of France. M. Goubet
declares emphatically : ' I have witnessed nothing
like what has been reported from Belgium. The
enemy progresses, doing no injury to the inhabitants beyond occasionally damaging property
where hospitality is refused. *They pay for all
food.*' " and everything else.

The Irish Future

There never was a war since the beginning of recorded time, which did not reek of atrocities, big and little. War is war, and war is hell. In regard to burning and **"A Blackened Wilderness."** devastation in war, no European nation has a cleaner record than England, yet a gentleman, who is now a Cabinet Minister, in *The Times History of the Transvaal War*, vol. v, pp. 158-65, and 254, wrote of " Lord Kitchener's scheme of universal devastation and depopulation," " organised pillage and destruction," "wholesale destruction and slaughter of cattle, sheep and horses." " A blackened wilderness," —not to mention mal-administered concentration camps, with 20,000 child victims. In America, Sherman's devastation of the Carolinas and Sheridan's of the Shenandoah Valley in 1865, were both more thorough and pitiless than in South Africa. Nothing that Germany did in Belgium and France was one-tenth part as terrible or systematic. " Military necessity," which we scoff at in German mouths, is, unfortunately, a very real thing. *Salus civitatis suprema lex.* British national security in 1807 necessitated our taking action to **Copenhagen.** prevent the Danish fleet falling into the hands of our powerful French enemy, and to enforce our demand we were compelled to bombard Copenhagen, the capital of a *neutral* nation, at peace with us, causing great loss of civilian lives and buildings.

The Germans have issued a big report describing

the atrocities committed on them by the Belgians. It, however, admits that many hundreds of Belgian civilians, mostly *francs-tireurs*, were shot by drum-head courts-martial. It was a hideous total, but the German armies were fighting for their lives. It is the essence of war that you are justified in killing every man who is trying to kill you, attacking from in front. What about attacking in the back? All honour to every man or woman who tries to destroy the invaders of the motherland, but they must take the dread consequences. The Italians did exactly the same thing as the Germans. Soon after they entered the war, Reuter's Agency reported : " In Tolmino and Friuli the Austrians have organised bodies of *francs-tireurs*. About 100 of these were caught red-handed with, besides arms, a large amount of Austrian money in their possession, for which they were unable to account. *They were shot.* This severe example, the evacuation of some villages and the manifestoes issued by the authorities threatening capital punishment for such offences have cleared the district." Lord Roberts gave short drift to the Boer horsemen who cut the railway in the rear of his advancing troops. Guerilla warfare knows no mercy and gives no quarter. The London *Standard* printed a Pretoria Dispatch dated 9th August 1900, which stated that " The Boers sniped a train at Bronkhurst yesterday on the line between Pretoria and Middleburg. Two of its occupants were wounded. In accordance with Lord Roberts's warning all the farms were fired within a radius of ten miles."

Very few writers on the earliest days of the War recognise how great was the service rendered by these brave Belgian civilian-soldiers, often led by their priests, as in Spain during Napoleon's invasion.

No Battle of
the Marne.

By all the laws of war the Germans were justified in shooting them when taken prisoner, for they were one of the chief causes of the German disaster on the Marne. The delay of food and munitions from Germany on the Belgian railways, due to their patriotic *sabotage*, rendered further German advance impossible. After the German retreat hundreds of German soldiers were found dead of starvation, their mouths red from the raw beet-root, which was the only food they could find. Indeed there was no Battle of the Marne, in the proper sense of battle, but a severe punishment of the German troops as they hurriedly retired. Field-Marshal Lord French, in his "1914," pp. 114-19, writes that before the battle "It was impossible for me to know the situation accurately in all its details. For instance, I could not then know, as I know now, that the Germans had abandoned their vigorous offensive twenty-four hours earlier than this, nor should I have conceived it possible." Naturally, inasmuch as it was not due to military failure or defeat. "I did not know at that time that a retreat had really set in." "In action early in the day,"— the first day of the British advance,—"it was discovered that a general retreat was in progress, covered by rearguards. On this I gave orders that the enemy was to be closely pressed." There was no battle on the Marne with the mass of the German Army, but a vigorous assault on its retreating rearguards. And that is an end of many French heroics, of General Manoury and his Paris taxi-cabs. The mortality was on both sides relatively small. " Our casualties were slight," writes Lord French.

As to the material devastation of Belgium, we now learn from no less an authority than the

"The Most Prosperous Country." late Lord Northcliffe that there was gross exaggeration. Writing in *The Times* of June, 1922, he stated : " There is an inclination in the mind of the public to exaggerate the amount of damage done to Belgium by the Germans. . . . The German Army lived in Belgium for years, spent money there and I say without hesitation that Belgium is the most prosperous country I have seen since I left New Zealand." No wonder. The Germans paid freely for everything they needed after the Belgian *francs-tireurs* stopped sniping at German soldiers by day and tearing up the railways by night. Many villages were shell-torn and burnt out, but the total damage was undoubtedly small considering the mighty war and vast armies that swept across her face.

After two and a half years of the German occupation of Belgium, that is, practically in the middle of the War, *The Times* of the 31st March,

1917, gave prominence to a vivid and " amazing picture " of Belgium, as seen by one of its correspondents, a Mr. J. P. Whitaker. After a tour through the villages between Brussels and Antwerp he found " no scarcity of good food." "Meat was plentiful, especially home-bred pork." So well fed was this gentleman that " I actually found myself gaining in flesh." " The Germans refrain from commandeering the Belgian supplies of food." " The natives are allowed to travel by railway without hindrance." " The policy of the Germans, in short, appears to be to interfere as little as possible with the everyday life of the country. The fruits of this policy are seen in a remarkable degree in Brussels. All day long the main streets of the city are full of bustle and all the outward manifestations of prosperity. Women in short fashionable skirts, with high-topped fancy boots, stroll completely at their ease along the pavement, studying the smart things, with which the drapers' shop windows are dressed. Jewellers' shops, provision stores, tobacconists and the rest show every sign of ' business as usual.' Even the sweetstuff shops had well-stocked windows. The theatres, music-halls, cinema palaces and cafés of Brussels were open and crowded." It seems to have been not half a bad thing to live in " tortured " Belgium under the Hun-Boche war administration.

The Germans acted in Belgium as they did in France in 1871-3. Marshal MacMahon, President of the French Republic, in a letter, dated the 4th September, 1873, to General Manteuffel, commanding the German army of occupation, wrote : " I deem it my duty to express to its Commander-in-Chief the sentiments which I experience on account of the justice and impartiality shown by him in the difficult mission which was entrusted to him."

"Justice and Impartiality."

How have French and Belgian officials and generals acted in the Ruhr towards hapless German men and women in times of peace ?

Louvain must be separately dealt with. Its ruined University, dear to every Irishman, is a horrible monument to the God of War. We have a clear statement of what occurred from a special correspondent of the *Daily Mail*, on 3rd September, 1914, Mr. A. J. Dawe, who was in the German lines from Brussels to Aix-la-Chapelle in disguise.

"A Veritable Fort."

" There can, of course, be no doubt that Louvain offered considerable resistance. The civic population, led by the Mayor and Belgian officers, worked machine guns upon the German trains as they approached the station, and the Church of St. Pierre, which overlooks the station, was turned into a veritable fort. The civilists fired upon the incoming troop trains from the windows and from behind the buttresses."

On the same day, 3rd September, on which the *Daily Mail* published Mr. Dawe's account, a distinguished war correspondent, Mr. Gerald Morgan, corroborated its facts in the *Daily*

The Irish Future

Telegraph in the course of a description of how nearly Brussels escaped from the consequences of a similar insurrection against the Germans by the civilian population. An eminent American writer, Mr. Richard Harding Davis, accompanied Mr. Morgan and honestly described the civilian warfare in American journals.

As a matter of fact, some German troops had been repulsed at Malines and had fallen back on Louvain in disorder. The citizens thought that the time had come to **"The Last Stand."** strike a patriotic blow for their country,—all honour to them. None were more brave than the students of the University, the buildings of which had become the centre of the rising, where also the last glorious stand was made. Many houses were burned in the street fighting.

The invasion of Eastern Prussia in the first week of war by the Russian armies was a real devastation like the Transvaal or **"Large Towns completely Sacked."** the Shenandoah Valley. Mr. Belloc, without a word of condemnation, estimated that the damage amounted in value to £20,000,000. The large town of Memel, bigger than Louvain, was burned to the ground, and the *Morning Post* gave its joyous approval in these words : " We are heartily glad that the Russians burned Memel and we hope that the Allies will burn a good many more German towns before this war is over." On the 23rd September, 1914, the London *Times* published a long account

213

from its war correspondent describing "the wholesale looting" of the German towns by the Russian soldiery. "Large towns have been completely sacked. The streets are covered with broken furniture, glass, and china from the plundered hourses. The Cossacks smash everything portable or detachable. They cover the roads with fragments of furniture, curtains, rugs, gramophones, inches deep." At the same time Reuter's telegrams recounted that "the Poles, Ruthenians and Jews, inhabiting the districts invaded by Russia, have already, some 70,000 of them, sought refuge in Vienna from the atrocities of the Russian soldiery." *The Times* made no mention in its leading articles of these evidences of Russian civilisation. Only Germany gives birth to Huns! War is war, and war is hell.

The world was horrified early in September, 1914, by this official statement of the French Government:

Rheims, an Official Lie. "Without being able to plead military exigencies, and solely for the pleasure of destruction, the German troops have subjected Rheims Cathedral to a systematic and furious bombardment."

Knowing what half a dozen shells would do, if there was any real intention to destroy a relatively fragile building like a church, the Press of Europe and America quite naturally assumed that the ancient and beautiful Cathedral had been levelled with the ground and burst unto a wild cry of execration against the criminals, who could be guilty of such an enormity. The lie got a splendid start and, though educated men soon learned the truth, you can still hear of this awful sacrilege of the German, Hun, and Vandal at ladies' tea parties in London and Washington.

The Cathedral was not injured by shell-fire but, in the words of a French officer, quoted in the London *Globe* of 22nd September, 1914, " at 2 p.m. on Sunday the Cathedral was badly damaged inside *Straw Fire not Shell-fire.* where some straw caught fire. Woodwork in the interior has been destroyed, but the Cathedral itself is not beyond repairing." The Paris correspondent of *The Times*, telegraphing on the 20th September, admitted that the German bombardment " appears to have been provoked "—by the fact that the " French planted their artillery in the city itself and replied to the enemy's guns with great vigour." There were several batteries in the great square in front of the Cathedral.

The *Westminster Gazette* of the 13th November 1915, confirmed the above statements in the words : " The Cathedral is not beyond repair. The outer wooden roof, which was needed to protect the stone roof from the weather, has been burned, but the Cathedral looks better without this ugly hump on its back. The stone roof, except for a small hole, is entirely as it was. A new roof will probably be made of slate and asbestos. Half of the celebrated orange window is broken, but much glass has been saved wherewith to repair it. *The two organs are untouched,*

as are the paintings, the pulpits, and the chapels ;
and the Cardinal goes very often to pray in his
private chapel. It was the burning of the straw,
on which German wounded were lying, that was
responsible for so much damage to the interior."
Writing as an eye-witness, Mr. Ward Price
narrated in the *Daily Mail* of 21st September,
how " the Abbé Andrieux, one of
A Wonderful Grand Stand. the Canons of the Cathedral, and
M. Guedet took me up the winding
staircase in the thick walls to the top of the high
Cathedral tower and I got a clear idea of the
battle." " The Cathedral tower was a wonderful
grand stand from which to watch this appalling
game of destruction." The Germans fired shrap-
nel several times at the tower to clear out the
French officers, *who were directing* the French
Artillery by their observations." Mr. Ward Price
added that, " one can hardly imagine that the
German gunners could miss so huge a mass as
Rheims Cathedral, towering as it did above the
town, if they had really wished to reach it." The
immunity of the great church is, no doubt, connected with the fact that the German soldiers
were South German corps, all Catholics, under the
command of the Catholic Duke Albrecht of Wur-
temburg. With a truthfulness that befits a great
churchman, Cardinal Luçon, Archbishop of
Rheims, in a letter to the *Echo de*
Walls Intact. *Paris,* dated the 27th September,
1914, stated that " the walls of the
edifice and the great organ are intact,"

The Irish Future

The last " atrocity " that I would ask my readers to consider is the alleged misuse of submarines in the destruction of mercantile ships. As I am not an expert in such mat- ters I leave it to those who ought to know what they are writing about. A fortnight before the War, Admiral Sir Percy Scott, in reply to some remarks by Lord Sydenham, considered the question fully in a letter in *The Times* of the 16th July, 1914. He first quoted the opinion of a foreign naval officer of " high experience," apparently French, on the law of submarine blockade to the following effect :

"Perfectly in Order."

" If we went to war with an insular country, depending for its food on supplies from overseas, it would be our business to stop that supply. On the declaration of war we should notify the enemy that she should warn those of her merchant ships coming home not to approach the island, as we were establishing a blockade of mines and submarines. Similarly we should notify all neutrals that such a blockade had been established, and that if any of their vessels approached the island they would be liable to destruction either by mines or submarines, and therefore would do so at their own risk." *This is exactly what the Germans did.* Sir Percy Scott agreed absolutely with this opinion and proceeded :

" Such a proclamation would, in my opinion, be *perfectly in order*, and once it had been made if any British or neutral ships disregarded it they could not be held to be engaged in the peaceful

217

avocations referred to by Lord Sydenham, and
if they were sunk in the attempt, it could not be
described as a relapse into savagery or piracy in
its blackest form. If Lord Sydenham will look
up the accounts of what usually

American Example. happened to the blockade-runners
into Charleston during the Civil War
in America, I think he will find that the block-
ading cruisers seldom had any scruples about
firing into the vessels they were chasing or driving
them ashore, and even peppering them when
stranded with grape and shell. The mine and the
submarine torpedo will be newer deterrents."

The history of naval warfare is full of such
incidents, and an Admiral who allowed a merchant ship loaded with ammunition or food to
escape would run a risk of being shot on his own
quarter-deck after court-martial.

Infinitely more important, however, are the
statements of Admiral Lord Fisher made in a

"She Must Sink Her Captures." special article in *The Times* of the
26th November, 1919, a year *after
the War* had ended, which afterwards
were reproduced by him in a book, entitled
Records. He lays down the principle that, " the
essence of war is violence and that moderation
in war is imbecility." Von Tirpitz could not be
more plain spoken. He developed his arguments
in regard to " Submarines and Commerce " in
these words :

" Again, the question arises as to what a submarine can do against a merchant ship when she

has found her. She cannot capture the merchant ship ; she has no spare hands to put a prize crew on board. Harmless trader in appearance, in reality she may be one of the numerous fleet auxiliaries, a mine-layer, or carrying troops, and so on." Field-Marshal Lord Grenfell in his *Memoirs*, published in the *Morning Post* on the 23rd October, 1926, condemning an official report published in India, remarked : " To publish such a report in the middle of a great war was the greatest possible political mistake, and the Germans got much valuable information out of it, especially the fact that ammunition was carried in what are called Hospital Ships, the real fact being that wounded soldiers, supplies, and ammunition were all forwarded together. Hospital ships were apparently not properly organised till after the War Office had taken over the direction of the campaign. It was a lamentable case of dirty linen being washed in public." " The apparent merchant ship," continued Lord Fisher, " may also be armed. In this light, indeed, the recent arming of our British merchantmen is unfortunate, for it gives the hostile submarine an excellent excuse (if she needs one) for sinking them,—namely, that of self-defence against the guns of the merchant ship. What can be the answer to all the foregoing but that (barbarous and inhuman as, we again repeat, it may appear), if the submarine is used at all against commerce, *she must sink her captures* ? "

" She must sink her captures." War is war,

and war is hell. All war is barbarous and inhuman. " Moderation in war is imbecility." Infinitely the most inhuman act of war is the blockade, which avowedly is not aimed at soldiers or sailors, but at the aged and the child, the babe and the woman. In the Middle Ages the Catholic Church inflicted the major excommunication on any general who blockaded a town before he had given full opportunity for the withdrawal of women and children. In those uncivilised days there was such a thing as " The Truce of God."

Pope Benedict XV, in condemning the sinking of the *Lusitania,* said ; " I know no more frightful crime. How distressing to see our generation a prey to such horrors ! But do you think the blockade which hems two Empires and condemns millions of innocents to famine is prompted by very humane sentiments ? "

A further question arises as to whether the German submarines carried out their odious duties in an especially " inhuman " **"Legitimate and Humane."** manner. So strong, so explicit were the allegations that I, like every Briton, believed that the charge was only too true. During my recent visit to the United States I quite accidentally picked up a monthly review for June, 1923, called *Current History,* published by the New York Times Company, and noticed that the first article was entitled " Rear-Admiral Sims on U-Boat Atrocities, Champions Submarines." I knew Admiral Sims to be as pro-British as the whole of the Pilgrims'

The Irish Future

Club rolled together, the nearest approach to a full-blooded John Bull that the United States could produce. Two of the first sentences of this striking article declared that, in condemning submarine warfare, " The United States are deprived by the Naval Treaty (of Washington) of a *legitimate and humane* method of destroying an enemy's commerce," and that, " one of the aims of this article is to correct the impression that all German naval officers were habitually guilty of acts of savage cruelty."

The evidence of Admiral Sims is peculiarly valuable in regard to submarines, as it was his special duty on arriving in England to devise measures, in co-operation with Admiral Jellicoe, to defeat their " terribly destructive " operations. I make a few quotations from this article :

(*i*) " War-stimulated hatred has created the belief that the common practice of the German submarine commanders was not only simply to murder the crews of the merchant ships torpedoed, but to do so with all the savage cruelty they could conceive of. There were attributed to these officers by honest people many atrocities of such an inhuman and revolting nature, that in normal times one would consider them beyond the possibility of belief by any persons not still suffering from war monomania. I have met many such people who, though normally thoughtful and kindly Christians, **" Awful Yarns."** honestly believe these *awful yarns*.

(*ii*) " Ever since my return from the War in

April, 1919, I have tried to make the significance of the submarine clear to our people. I have explained it in untechnical terms to more than *one hundred audiences*, also in a popular account in a book of several hundred pages and in a number of articles, but apparently without much success in making it really understood. *The Press has appeared to be unwilling to publish the facts.*"

The Press Conceals the Truth.

(*iii*) " Within the past few months, in speaking to various audiences on the operations of the German submarines, I have stated that their commanders were specially selected and thoroughly trained men, and that most of the accounts of atrocities popularly attributed to them were untrue. The submarine commanders generally acted in a humane manner in carrying out the orders of their Government, in some instances giving the boats of torpedoed merchant vessels *food and water* and a tow toward land, and sending out wireless signals giving their position."

"Food and Water."

It took many years before the American Press published these well-authenticated facts.

CHAPTER XIII

THE SUPREME QUESTION OF INDIA

(i) " The Government assessment does not leave enough food to the cultivator to support himself and his family throughout the year."—

Sir William Hunter, K.C.S.I.,
the Historian of India, in the
Viceroy's Council, 1883.

(ii) " There is no more pathetic figure in the British Empire than the Indian peasant. His masters have ever been unjust to him. He is ground until everything has been expressed, except the marrow of his bones."—

Mr. Herbert Compton,
in *Indian Life*, 1904.

(iii)

They are slaves who fear to speak
For the fallen and the weak;
They are slaves who will not choose
Hatred, scoffing and abuse
Rather than in silence shrink
From the truth they needs must think;
They are slaves who dare not be
In the right with two or three.

J. R. Lowell, U.S. Ambassador
to London in 1880.

223

The Irish Future

I HAVE introduced this chapter into a book where it certainly seems out of place, because its subject-matter has been neglected by both the great parties of the State, Conservative and Liberal, and I seek the earliest opportunity to appeal to the New National Government in the hope of redress. Moreover, at my age I cannot write another book on the Indian peasantry, *their misery and famines*, a supreme grievance, to which I have devoted over half a century of my life.

I fear I was at times an annoyance to those in high places in India, and I don't blame them for sending me to backward and un-"Scrupulous Moderation." healthy districts, for I had the honour and great pleasure of gaining the approval of two Secretaries of State for India, the Marquis of Hartington and Lord Randolph Churchill, the latter insisting on my being stationed to Darjeeling, the healthiest part of Bengal. The Anglo-Indian Press recognised "the scrupulous moderation" of my books. In after years, when I was in Parliament, two other Secretaries of State for India recommended me for a knighthood, which Mr. Asquith, as Prime Minister, though the Chief Liberal Whip supported my claim, promptly vetoed. I should have appreciated the distinction as a recognition of work, which the India Office found good. A baronetcy was the reward of an Indian civilian who distinguished himself in Parliament as the bitter exponent of hostility to every Indian reform.

The Irish Future

No doubt a very appreciable part of the unrest in India is due to an awakening sense of fitness for self-government amongst the educated classes. There are thousands of Indians who have received a thorough training in every branch of knowledge, and resent the importation every year from England of a group of very able young men, who, on the strength of a competitive examination, become a governing power, whose decisions are omnipotent. I was for nearly thirty years a member of this very distinguished body, and that fact has been the pride and joy of my life. The Indian Civil Service was the most perfect engine of administration and justice that a government based on conquest ever evolved and, as an Irishman, I often wished that its excellencies could be transferred to my western home, but it had two weaknesses—one that it was exotic, wholly foreign to Indian traditions, and therefore ephemeral, and, secondly, that it was very expensive in a very poor country and a main cause of heavy taxation.

Exotic though Excellent.

It would be impossible to discuss with any fullness the very numerous questions that must arise in the administration of an empire, the population of which runs into hundreds of millions. The Special Committee, known as the Simon Commission, is now dealing with a portion of these awkward topics and, to my mind, not the most urgent or important portion. The form of

Courage and Honesty.

constitution best suited for India's needs is, beyond doubt, a subject worthy of high statesmanship, but the condition of the Indian peoples and its amelioration is far and away the most clamant, and demands courage and honesty in Calcutta and Simla rather than forensic or literary displays in Parliament or at the India Office.

I practically began my service in India as First Assistant to Sir William W. Hunter, K.C.S.I., Director General of Statistics, an **A Sympathetic Scotchman.** office that afforded me exceptional opportunities for studying the inside of Indian questions. This distinguished man, afterwards the Historian of India, was one of the large group of very capable and sympathetic Scotchmen, who, with an equally numerous body of Irishmen, applied Celtic kindliness to the government of a vast agricultural population. Recruitment to the Civil Service was in later years arranged to the advantage of English students from Oxford, and I do not think that Indian administration became, as was deeply needed, more sympathetic or wise in dealing with an awakening nationalist feeling. Sir W. Hunter pressed on the Supreme Government what ought to have been its supreme task, the betterment of the farmer and the villager. I was able to back up his views by a book, entitled *The Ruin of an Indian Province*, which had the honour of being the basis of a full and important debate in the House of Commons by a few altruistic members, whose voices never reached the British public, at the time fully engaged in the great struggle over the Irish Rent Laws.

A few years later, in 1903, I was able to renew the struggle for the Indian peasant in *The Failure of Lord Curzon*, who, in his imperialistic atmosphere, seems never **50 per cent. Income Tax.** to have had a thought for the lowly husbandman, whose taxes paid for his high-born ambitions. I had the great advantage of the support of a very distinguished body of Indian Civil Servants, who in 1901 petitioned the Secretary of State for India for some restriction on the ceaseless enhancements of the Land Tax. They were Sir Richard Garth, late Chief Justice of the High Court of Calcutta, Sir John Jardine, late Judge of the High Court of Bombay, Sir Henry Cotton, Governor of Assam, Sir William Wedderburn, M.P., and eight others of the highest official rank. Their petition may be summarised in a sentence. They prayed that the demand of land revenue should not exceed one-half of the net profit of each estate or farm, that is, that it should not exceed a 50 per cent. income tax !

There has been during the past year serious trouble in the Bombay Presidency, and a threatened strike against land taxation at a place called Bardoli, where an increase of 35 per cent. in land tax was demanded. Things, in fact, had not improved much since 1877, when serious anti-tax riots swept across the Bombay Province. This seems a long time ago, but, as Bardoli proves, increased taxation still continues, though its effects nowadays rarely come to the surface. The Government in 1878 wisely and justly appointed a commission of inquiry, and its report was terribly outspoken and truthful. The *Pioneer*, the leading journal of India and the most Conservative, the organ, in fact, of the British Government, summarised it in these words :

"The final element of distress that broke the ryots' heart must be looked for in the revised land revenue assessments, in them-
"Bereft of All Hope." selves extravagantly heavy. The enhancements made at the recent revision were, judging by all known standards, excessive. Viewed in conjunction with the status of those, on whom they were imposed they were *ruinous*. They ranged in different sub-districts from 33 to 66 per cent. On individual villages they were often doubled ; on individual holdings they were *constantly* more than doubled." One distinguished Bombay officer, Sir George Wingate, did not mince matters : "What must have been the state of things," he angrily exclaimed, "which can compel cultivators, proverbially patient and long-suffering, accustomed to more or less of ill-usage and injustice at all times, to redress their wrongs by murder, and in defiance of an ignominious death to themselves ? How must their sense of justice have been violated ? How must they have been bereft of all hope of redress from law or Government before their patient and peaceful natures could be roused to

the point of desperation required for such a deed ? " .

" A more damning indictment," continued the *Pioneer*, " was never recorded against a civilised government. Stupidity, blindness, indifference, greed—inability, in a word, in all its thousand forms— **"Not Enough Food."** settled down, like the fabled harpies, on the ryot's bread, and bore off with them all that he subsisted upon."

This is exactly what Sir William Hunter said in the Viceroy's Council. " The Government assessment does not leave enough food to the cultivator to support himself and his family throughout the year. '

The next scene of destructive famine was in Madras, and the *Englishman* of Calcutta, another Conservative journal, mildly suggested that " the husbandmen were less able to bear the strain of bad seasons, *in consequence of the enormous increase in the revenue taken from them.*" It had recorded that " twenty years of British rule have increased the Government demand upon the agriculture of Madras by one million rupees."

Another high official, the Hon. Mr. G. Rogers, of the Indian Civil Service, and Member of the Bombay Council, writing to the Under-Secretary of State for India, **850,000 Heads of Families.** declared : " In the eleven years from 1879-80 to 1889-90 there were sold by action for the collection of land revenue the occupancy rights (the leases) of 1,963,364 acres of land held by 840,713 defaulters, in addition to *personal* property of the value of Rs. 29,65,081. Of the 1,963,364 acres, 1,174,143 had to be bought in on the part of Government for want of bidders, that is to say, very nearly 60 per cent. of the land suppposed to be fairly and equitably assessed could not find purchasers, and only the balance of 779,142 acres was sold. The evils of the Mahratta farming system (in Bombay) have been pointed out in my *History of the Bombay Land Revenue,* but I doubt if that system at its worst could have shown such a spectacle as that of nearly 850,000 ryots (heads of families) in the course of eleven years sold out of about 1,900,000 acres of land." *Roundly one-eighth part of the entire agricultural population of the Madras Presidency was sold out of house and home in a little more than a decade. Not only were their farms brought to auction, but their poor personal belongings, their plough cattle and their cooking utensils, their beds and everything but their scanty clothes were sold to provide money for mostly "Imperialistic" adventure.* The picture is incomplete till it is remembered that these eleven years of " denudation " immediately followed the terrible famine of 1877-78, during which Madras lost three millions of its inhabitants by starvation. I do not blame very much the revenue officials. They were hard-working men, loyally carrying out strict orders and the well-considered policy of their governments.

It will be urged that this is ancient history, and I reply that the writing and publishing of outspoken reports is ancient history. With fifty years' close acquaintance with Indian affairs I say most positively that this enormous grievance is, as it was in **The Cause of Sedition.** Ireland, the chief cause of discontent and even sedition. The great mass of the so-called agitators are the sons of farmers. A few years ago the Hon. B. K. Bose, a Member of the Viceroy's Council, stood up in the presence of Lord Curzon and stated that : " Proceedings in the Central Provinces with a view to a second new Settlement are in progress in Bilaspur and Raipur. These districts, especially the former, were very hard hit during the last famine. They are no less so this time. They were both newly assessed only *about ten years ago* ! The enhancement in Bilaspur was 102 per cent. in some groups and 105 per cent. in others." And there was no denial. "The Great Viceroy" and his Council sat silent. Did they even listen ? At the time their thoughts were far away, considering " Imperialist " schemes for railways into Persia and China. Other districts were hardly less severely dealt with. The enhancement on the previous revenue demand was in some groups of villages in Saugor District, 68 and 53 per cent. ; in Jubbulpore District, 86 and 50 per cent. ; in Seoni District, 97 and 92 per cent. ; in Hoshungabad District, 96 and 69 per cent., and in Raipur District 98 per cent. Moreover, the currency or term of the settlement was shortened from thirty to twenty years. The population of the Central

The Irish Future

Provinces decreased by a million in the decade ending 1900. Is there any evidence that the land taxes have been since then reduced? The military budget increased between the years 1875 and 1900 from roundly 120 millions to 230 millions of rupees, whilst the total debt of India went up from £95,000,000 to £199,00,000, the increase being chiefly due to wars on the North-West Frontier and the relief of famine, aggravated by taxation.

It makes very little difference to 300,000,000 of Indian peasants what the Simon Commission may recommend, but I fear that the ryot will remain "the most pathetic figure in the British Empire" for "his masters have ever been unjust to him" and Christendom will have one more failure to its discredit.

"The Most Pathetic Figure."

CHAPTER XIV

THE CELTIC EMPIRE OF GREAT BRITAIN

THE ANGLO-SAXON MYTH.

"Myths die hard, but the 'Anglo-Saxon' myth is very nearly dead. The anthropological evidence of the Celtic origin of the people of England is clear, as has been pointed out by Beddoe, Huxley, Boyd-Dawkins, and other authorities. The archæological evidence is also definite."

Professor A. H. Sayce,
Queen's College, Oxford.

I HAVE included in my will a bequest for founding a scholarship of £500 a year at Oxford University, Edinburgh University, and the University of Wales, for the study of two questions, which should be most interesting to British people, viz.:

1. The British or Celtic element in the existing population of England.
2. The British or Celtic element in the English language and the dialects of English counties.

The great scholar, Sir John Rhys, Professor of Celtic at Oxford, gave me full encouragement, adding that " a considerable amount of new material

has been accumulated " and needed examination.
The use of the word " British " instead of
" English " has become very common and is
understood to be due to a regard for Scotch
and Welsh susceptibilities, but it
would have a more real foundation
if the history of Britain after
the Saxon Conquest and up to the time of the
Norman Conquest were studied without anti-
Celtic prejudices. The implications of Lord
Salisbury's sneer regarding " the Celtic fringe "
are still strong, although the words " the Saxon
fringe " are historically far more accurate. In
the following pages I give a few of the arguments
on the Celtic side, but questions, involving both
race and language, are too large for summary
discussion here. The scholarships I mention
above will, I hope, help towards a more careful
and wider study of the topics involved and the
British Englishman may come into his own at
last, as the Overlord of a great Celtic Confederacy.

The Saxon Fringe.

It rarely strikes even a well-educated Irishman
that the ordinary Englishman is as real a Celt as
himself. Still less often does the
very patriotic Briton, when proudly
singing that " Britons never, never
shall be slaves," remember that for centuries he
has proclaimed himself to be an Anglo-Saxon of
a mixed Germanic stock and thereby denied his
fatherland. If there is a well-established fact in
early English history it is that the British population of England was a very large one, when the

"Britons Never Shall be Slaves."

234

The Irish Future

harassed Romans withdrew from its shores, and that it had supplied tens of thousands of soldiers to the Roman armies. Constantine's victory of the Labarum, which, in A.D. 312, established the Christian religion in the Roman Empire, was won by British legionaries. Centuries of Roman culture had left their mark, and in the fifth century Britain, like Ireland, was high placed amongst civilised peoples. Hume in his *History of England* states that, " Under the Roman dominion Britain had assumed an aspect of great prosperity." " Agriculture was **Roman Culture.** carried to such a pitch that the island not only fed itself, but also exported large quantities of grain to the northern provinces of the Empire." Beda speaks of Roman towns, lighthouses, roads and bridges existing in his time. The large towns, like York, Chester, Bath, and Lincoln had their " theatres, temples, circuses, baths, and palaces." " Thus when the Saxons established themselves in Britain they must have dwelt within Roman walls and feasted their eyes with the magnificent works of Roman Art." In 429, when St. Germanus, Bishop of Auxerre, visited Britain he found the country prosperous and wealthy.

If we are to believe the Anglo-Saxon maniacs this vast population and high civilisation was destroyed by the Teutonic invasion. These invading Germans may have **British Wives.** been Huns or Boches, but they were not fools and indeed had a considerable civilisa-

tion of their own. They may have burned much
and killed many, but they knew, as their race
brethren in France did, that a conquered population of skilled farmers was a very valuable form
of spoil. There is no evidence of slaughter, except
in battle, but there was a cruel slavery. In his
valuable book on *Middlesex in British, Roman,
and Saxon Times*, Mr. Montague Sharpe, after
describing how the Saxons adopted the elaborate
Roman land survey of Britain in its entirety,
adds : " It was not to the advantage of the
Saxons, (who took over a century to subjugate
Britain), to destroy the long-established agricultural system of the Romano-British, on which
the sustenance of both conqueror and conquered
depended, and it is interesting to note how much
of it is to be found existing down to the time of
the enclosure of parishes," a couple of centuries
ago. Only their chiefs and captains brought
women with them and the Saxon soldiery found
wives from British homes, probably by violence.
The atlas appended to the *History of England* by
Mr. S. R. Gardiner, the distinguished historian,
shows in Map 3, how small were
The Celtic Survival. the Saxon settlements in 550
after a hundred years of invasion,
not one-tenth part of the island. As late as 626
an independent British Kingdom existed round
Leeds and in the following decade a British Confederacy very nearly drove the Saxons out of
England. It is difficult to explain how Caedwalla,
King of the West Saxons in 685, came by his purely

The Irish Future

Cymbric name. The eighth-century historian, Bede, speaks of the British having " submitted themselves to the enemy and passed into servitude," which lasted till William of Normandy came in the eleventh century to give them freedom. The conquest was slow, because the invaders were relatively few in number, so few that we find them grouping themselves in hundreds or *wapentakes* for military defence against the large British servile population, amidst which they lived. These hundreds were numerous only on the east coast where the Angles and Saxons first settled, as centuries later the English formed the Pale out of a few eastern counties in Ireland.

The almost instantaneous submission of England to its Norman Conquerors is explicable only on the hypothesis that they were welcomed by the great British serf **Massacre or Flight.** population. The Saxons continued the struggle for only a very few months and were driven from their homes by the Norman nobility leading British armies. They were massacred mercilessly, and Hume in describing the devastation, " of the fertile country for sixty miles between the Humber and the Tees," where the Saxon inhabitants were most numerous, mentions that, " the lives of 100,000 persons were computed to have been sacrificed to this barbarous stroke." All over broad England the same hideous clearance was carried out. Being in a marked minority, the Saxon masters of Britain could not save themselves, except by flight. In the words of the *Anglo-Saxon Chronicle* " the King, William, with all the force he could collect "—certainly Britons—" went northward, despoiling and laying waste." The Norman army had been largely recruited from Brittany and the Celtic provinces of Anjou and Aquitaine, which used British or Cymric dialects. Within a quarter of a century Anglo-Saxon names almost disappeared from England. Gone the Ethelreds, the Alfrics, the Elfgars, the Cynewolds, the Edrics, the Morcars, the Osrics, the Sihtrics and a **The Anglo-Saxons Decimated.** hundred other names that fill the *Anglo-Saxon Chronicle.* They fled to Scotland and the Continent, even to far Constantinople, where they formed a large part of the Varangian body-guard of the Emperor. Their place was taken by Howards (Hogwards), Stewards (Stywards), Shepherds (Sheepwards), Fishers, Butchers, Coopers, Websters and the old servile race of British. The Anglo-Saxon was gone or hid himself under an assumed name, leaving behind him little except his simple, flexible and admirable language, probably the most perfect form of speech known to mankind, which in a few generations displaced the French of the new Norman overlords, as it had vanquished the old Cymric speech of Britain. In after centuries it was to displace the Gaelic of Ireland and the many tongues of the polyglot peoples of the United States. The Saxon race for the most part disappeared and the Briton, as Celtic as the Scot or the Welshman, started out to found the

greatest empire in history. It is a very significant
fact that the most powerful of the Anglo-Saxon
Kings assumed the title of Bretwalda, or Weilder
of the Britons, to signify the supremacy that he
claimed.

It may be interesting to examine in a few words
what overwhelming evidence of British survival
is to be found in the language we
speak and in the many county **Domestic and Homely Words.**
dialects that still survive in Great
Britain. As long ago as 1855 the *Transactions
of the Philological Society* put on record these
facts, " If an ' Anglo-Saxon ' calls for his *coat* or
tells of the *basket* of fish he has caught or the *cart*
he employs on his land or the *pranks* of his youth
or the *prancing* of his horse or declares that he is
happy or that his servant is *pert* or affirms that
an assertion is *balderdash* or a claim a *sham*, like
the M. Jourdain of Molière, who had been talking
prose all his life without knowing it, he has been
speaking very good Celtic without any suspicion
of the fact." " A considerable proportion of the
English words relating to the ordinary arts of
life, such as agriculture, carpentry and in general
indoor and outdoor service come from the Celtic."
A few are crock, mug, prop, hassock, taper, curds,
cub, ribbon, tag, skedaddle, spar (of a ship),
spigot, pike, sot, spank, harbour (from *aber*, a river
estuary), coal, clay, bran, cackle, gander, flannel,
gown, hem, lath, mattock, pail, pitcher, rein, puddle,
smug, udder, ridge, solder, tackle, wan, chortle,
rubbish, cur, knock, daddy, tread, rid, gnaw,

ford, muck, booth, crack, peak, fuddle, bug, louse, slim, odd, whiff, frail, dull, hog, puff, tub, coney, lawn, linnet, nanny, cheese—in all nearly two thousand of them, a very full vocabulary. I cannot go into dialect words of British origin, but they also number thousands. The *patois* of the " service " classes and of the peasantry down to the beginning of last century in every county from Yorkshire to Devon was, except for its English framework, mostly Celtic in noun and verb.

As a result of the preceding paragraphs I assert that the British Empire is, as its name suggests, a Celtic Empire, with every Celtic characteristic from the love of adventure to exceptional bravery and brilliancy of thought and language. Lord French said of the Irish regiments at Mons : " Years must elapse before the history of the Great War can be known and understood, but when that time arrives the part taken in it by the soldiers of Ireland will stand out nobly. They were always to be found where the fighting was most severe and Irish regiments stood their ground with a tenacity, which has never been surpassed in war." The same might be said of the soldiers of Devon or Yorkshire. I feel there was something Celtic and British in the generosity recorded by the Irishman, General Sir Charles Harrington : " Our men won the admiration of the Turks, because of the humanity they displayed, and our officers had in some cases to stop their men giving

British Bravery and Brains.

up their food to keep the poor (Greek) refugees alive." I shall be proud to be a Briton when Englishmen recognise their Celtic origin.

Were the Angles a Germanic tribe? It is doubtful. In German they appear as Angeln, and Ungëln, or rather Urgëln, latinised into Angli, the most important vowel being dropped. Ur, as in Urfürst, means original, primal and the " n " is simply a plural sign. Gël or Gael remains. We know that there was no territory called after the Angles in Germany, but that Celtic tribes in Germany were uprooted and driven north and west is an historic fact. Did one of them find its way to the east of Britain? The skulls in the cemeteries of Norfolk and Suffolk are of the long Celtic type and not like the round Teutonic crania.

The Origin of the Angles.

Whatever was the origin of the name of the Angeln, it is universally admitted that the Welsh were ancient Cymric Britons. The name Welsh gives no help as it is only a bit of Teutonic insolence. It is simply the German word Wälsch, meaning stranger or foreigner, and was applied by the Saxons to the Britons, exactly as the Austrians still apply it to the Italians. But where does Wales come from? There is no sign of it as a territorial entity in early Welsh Chronicles. Sir John Rhys, probably the greatest of Welsh scholars, in his *Welsh People* recognises that the Gaels had large settlements in Wales in pre-Christian times. They were the first wave of

Gaelic Wales.

Celts that passed over the face of Europe and were driven westward by the second wave, the Britons. They, however, left their name in Gaul or Gallia. Another branch founded Galatia in Asia Minor, where Celtic words are still found in the dialect of the villages. The Britons, the much larger section of the Celts, finally drove the Gaels into Ireland and Wales, where the mountains gave them a sanctuary down to Norman times. The interchange or combination of the letters G and W is very common in the Welsh language. Gwalia is the latinised form of Wales and Gladys or Gwladys is a well-known woman's name. This peculiarity is marked in surnames, such as Gwynn and Wynn, Guest and West, Woolland and Gulland. Gwylem, William and *Guillaume*, Gwatkin and Watkin, Guise and Wise, Gillett and Willett, Jebb and Webb, Wilmot and *Guillemot*, Wardrop and Garderobe. In fact Wales means the land of the Gaels. Perhaps our Irish friends may feel more friendly to the Briton when he knows that the King's eldest son bears the proud title of Prince of Gaels.

The ancient name of Ireland was Ierne, latinised into Ivernia. How came it that the English called its people Scots down to the **The Runaway Scots.** end of the eleventh century and even extended the name to the people of Caledon, the Black Mountains, when the Northern Irish conquered Scotland about the fifth century? There is a fable that there was an Irish Queen named Scotia, but it has no foundation in fact. The most probable origin is that it is a term of abuse, like Slav, and means the Scouters or Runaways. The Irish had an evil practice of raiding the coasts of Britain and France, but were careful to bolt with their plunder before their victims could assemble and punish the marauders. Old Irish records are full of accounts of these piracies. It is a wonderful feat of human speech that this name has degenerated in England into the grossity of calling a man a scut, whilst in North Britain, it has been raised, as Scotch, by a virile race to a place of special pride and honour. The absorption of the Pictish Caledon into the Irish Empire was thorough. The Hon. R. Erskine of Marr, writing in *The Times* a few months ago, states that :

" The vast majority of Scottish place-names, whether Highland or Lowland, is Celtic or pre-Celtic. When the feudal system was introduced into the Lowlands of Scotland in the reign of David I, the vernacular was Gaelic, and Gaelic remained the vernacular in many parts of the Lowlands until some time after 1745. Broadly speaking, there is no racial distinction between Highlanders and Lowlanders, but one of language and manners and customs only." One specially adventurous Irishman forced his way to the borders of England and his descendants remain to this day, the Scotts, Dukes of Buccleuch, " the bold Buccleuch." In a couple of centuries the Scot of North Britain threw off the overlordship of the Irish Kings and set up a very vigorous kingdom of his own. It is impossible to deny that the Scot is by origin an Irish Gael and a splendid type of the race. Nicknames survived in ancient days more readily than now. The Campbells and the Camerons, the Crooked Mouths and Crooked Noses, are branches of an old-world Irish Sept.

Nor can one overlook, in considering the population of England, the enormous immigrations from Wales, Scotland, and Ireland **The Immigrant Celt.** in recent centuries. They must run into many millions. We have all heard of the ubiquitous Scot and the Welsh are even more numerous. Since the days of the Tudors—the Welsh form of Theodore—and the Cecils—Welsh Cyssels, as *Burke's Peerage* recognises—Welshmen have flooded into England. Half Lancashire and South London are practically settlements of Irishmen, who now number in Great Britain 2,000,000.

Count Maxmilian O'Donnell, of Vienna, Son of Field-
Marshal Count Maurice O'Donnell.

CHAPTER XV

THE LAST PRINCELY FAMILY OF IRELAND

FRANK HUGH O'DONNELL

Sacred the Cause O'Donnell's defending,
  The altars we kneel at and homes of our sires ;
Ruthless the ruin the foe is extending,
  Midnight is red with the plunderer's fires.

Wildly o'er Desmond the war wolf is howling,
  Fearless the eagle sweeps over the plain,
The fox in the streets of the city is prowling,
  All, all who could scare them are banished or slain.

O'Donnell Abu (A.D. 1597)
translated by M. J. McCann.

An ignorant practice has grown up of describing
the chiefs of Irish clans as kings, suggesting that
they were independent rulers of many
petty principalities. They were, **Four Princely Families.**
as in Scotland, simply noblemen
of more or less exalted rank in a United Kingdom,
above whom stood the Ard Righ or sole sovereign,
ruling the whole island from Tara in Meath. For
centuries this high office was held by the royal
family of O'Neill, round whom were grouped the

four princely provincial overlords, the O'Donnells
in Ulster, the O'Briens in Munster, the O'Conors
in Connaught and the O'Kavanaghs in Leinster.
The last of these four families practically disappeared soon after the Conquest by Henry II in
1272 and their confiscated territories became the
Pale or English settlement round Dublin. Munster
and Connaught were overrun in the following
century, and, though their princely houses survived down to the Reformation, they were
dominated by a few great Norman noblemen,
Fitzgeralds, Butlers and De Burgos or Burkes,
who in time became "more Irish than the Irish
themselves." The O'Neills and O'Donnells pre-
served their independence in Ulster with almost
undiminished vigour for over three centuries, down
to their defeat at the beginning of the seventeenth
century at the battle of Kinsale. Since then the
O'Neills have disappeared almost as thoroughly
as the O'Kavanaghs, the last of them in Ireland,
according to Sir Bernard Burke's *Vicissitudes of
Families*, being a sergeant in a British regiment,
while Henry O'Neill, Marquis de la Granja in Spain,
dying without issue a couple of decades ago, was the
only known survivor on the Continent in our day.

The disappearance of the three sons of Hugh
O'Neill, the last Earl of Tyrone, and of their heirs,
is one of the unsolved mysteries of Irish History.
The youngest was undoubtedly murdered in his
bedroom by an unknown assassin in Belgium but
there is no known cause for the early deaths of the
other two. The publication of *State Papers* con-

nected with the Elizabethan period, chiefly the *Carew Papers* 1559-1600, shows that the taking off of Irish noblemen of great rank was a favourite practice, organised in England. For instance, a despatch of the great William Cecil, Lord Burghley and Lord High Treasurer, gives instructions to Sir George Carew, Lord President of Munster, as to the removal of the young Earl of Desmond. " Take this from me," wrote Cecil, " that whatever you do to abridge him shall never be imputed to you as a fault." The Viceroy, the Earl of Sussex, sent out assassins, broadcast, against John, Earl of Tyrone, against MacHugh O'Byrne, Lord Glenmalure, and against Lord Hugh O'Neill. These failed but the plot against Hugh O'Donnell, Earl of Tyrconnell at Valladolid in Spain was successful. In May 1682, a miscreant, named James Blake, of Galway, came to the Lord President and offered to follow Red Hugh into Spain. Carew approved the plot and wrote to the Viceroy, Lord Mountjoy, " God give him strength and perseverance." " I told him I would acquaint your lordship with it." In October the news of O'Donnell's death at Valladolid reached Ireland and Carew wrote again to Mountjoy, gloating over the event thus : " O'Donnell is dead and I do think that it will fall out that he has been poisoned by James Blake, of whom your lordship has been formerly acquainted." The Earl of Sussex wrote to Queen Elizabeth on the 24th August 1561, in regard to the would-be murderer of O'Neill, that " I bound myself by my oath to see him have 100 marks of land. I told him the ways he might do it and how to escape after with safety." A most efficient Viceroy.

It may be good for the rising hopes of Irishmen to learn in some detail what the last princely family of our race has done and is doing *A Cardinal and a Duke.* to-day. Within the last few years two of its members have gained the highest distinction, His Eminence the Most Reverend Patrick O'Donnell of Raphoe becoming Cardinal Archbishop of Armagh and Primate of Ireland, whilst His Excellency Don Juan O'Donnell, Duke of Tetuan, was Secretary of State in the War Ministry of Spain. The latter was specially selected for his high office by General Primo de Rivera because of the great influence he and his forefathers have had with the Spanish Army. He was, in fact, the right-hand man of that great Reformer in his attack on the corrupt administrations that preceded him and had brought the fair name of Spain so low.

There was, however, a much more distinguished O'Donnell in the person of Leopold O'Donnell who won the title of Duc de Tetuan for his conquests in Northern Africa about 1855. Among the Irish nobility, who fled to Spain *A Regent of Spain.* after the battle of the Boyne in 1689 was Hugh O'Donnell of Murrisk in County Mayo. He became a General in the Spanish army and settled in Andalusia, from whom in the fourth generation sprang Leopold O'Donnell, Count de Lucana. He placed Queen Isabella on the throne in 1843 and maintained her there for over a quarter of a century. In 1860 he conquered Morocco and was created Duke of Tetuan. Since the preceding year he had been Prime Minister and held that office nearly to his death in 1868. His uncle, General Charles O'Donnell, Count La Bisbal, Director-General of Artillery, was for a time one of the three Regents appointed by the Cortes to govern Spain after the dethronement of Ferdinand VII by the great Napoleon in 1808. His nephew, Charles, the second Duke of Tetuan, was President of the Senate in 1882 and Ambassador at Vienna.

As in Spain, the most distinguished Generals in Austria of Irish origin sprang from the same noble Ulster family. The founder of the line was Count Charles O'Don- **The V.C. of the Austrian Empire.** nell born in Ireland in 1715, General of Cavalry and Grand Cross of the Order of Maria Theresa, the highest honour an Austrian soldier can attain to. It is equivalent to the Victoria Cross and given only for acts of the most daring bravery. It is very peculiar in one respect, in that it is not conferred by the Sovereign or the War Ministry, but by its own chapter, that is, by the vote of the great soldiers, who already have won its almost unattainable distinction. Its holders are few and the family of O'Donnell in Austria is the only one, on which it has been conferred three times. That Count Charles deserved it there can be no doubt. He was wounded in the wars against the Turks and advanced rapidly in his career, being Colonel of the cuirassier regiment of Cordova at the age of 27 and General at 41. He was again wounded at the battle of Kollin, fighting against the Prussians, and at the great battle of Torgau in 1760 commanded five regiments of Cavalry. Early in the day the Austrian commander-in-chief, Marshal Daun, was wounded and his army began to retreat, but O'Donnell hurled his cavalry against the advancing Prussians, under the Great Frederick, leading it himself, and drove them back, thus enabling the Austrian infantry to withdraw in safety. He made a prisoner of the Prussian General Furkenstein and in the morning retired in perfect order. He was Governor of the Netherlands in 1762.

The next O'Donnell of great distinction was Field-Marshal Count John, who distinguished himself in the Seven Years' War against Prussia and also received the Grand Cross of the Order of Maria Theresa.

Major-General Count Henry O'Donnell was born in Castlebar in County Mayo in 1726 and fought against Prussia in the Austrian Wars of Succession. He was so badly wounded at Schweidnitz that he retired and afterwards married Leopoldine, Princess Cantacuzene of the Imperial family of the Paleologi of Constantinople, a near relative of the Empress Maria Theresa.

Their son, Count Joseph O'Donnell, born in 1756, became the famous Finance Minister of the Emperor Joseph II and was President **A Great Finance Minister** of the Upper House. He stemmed the financial ruin that the Napoleonic invasions brought and saved the Austrian Exchequer from collapse. Governor of Carinthia and Adjutant-General for War, Grand Cross of the Order of St. Stephen.

His son, Field-Marshal Count Maurice O'Donnell, lived in times of peace, but rose to the highest position in the Army. He was known for his good looks, and married Princess Christine of the noble Belgian family of De Ligne, a famous beauty of the Napoleonic era.

His son, Count Maximilian O'Donnell, became the most well-known member of his family for saving the life of the Emperor Franz Joseph in 1852, a deed rewarded by the extraordinary grant of the right **A Forgotten Hero** to carry on his heraldic shield the arms of the House of Hapsburg quartered with those of O'Donnell. He was on duty as aide-de-camp with the young Emperor, when an assassin rushed on him with a knife. Unable to stop the would-be murderer, O'Donnell, little more than a boy, threw himself in between, receiving the knife in his own shoulder. The Emperor was also slightly wounded, and Max O'Donnell, forgetting his own grievous wound, sucked the wound of the Emperor to prevent the danger of poison. A magnificent Votive Chapel was built in Vienna, subscribed to by the Sovereigns and great nobles of Europe. Yet when I visited it three years ago the name of Max O'Donnell had been forgotten even by the vergers of the Chapel. As in Rome, where the tombs of the Ulster Princes, O'Neil and O'Donnell, are neglected by the modern Irish,

The Irish Future

so the name of the Irish-Austrian hero has passed away from memory within three quarters of a century.

Three Counts O'Donnell of the rank of Major gave their lives for Austria in the Napoleonic Wars : Count Hugh at Neerwinden, Count Charles at Kehl, and another Charles at Aspern.

In the United States two O'Donnells deserve mention. John O'Donnell of Baltimore, the most Irish town in the Union, had an **From Calcutta to Baltimore.** extraordinary career. When a boy he ran away from his home, Truagh Castle, County Limerick, to Calcutta, where he landed penniless, but before he was thirty he had amassed a great fortune. He was anxious to discover a new route to the East through Northern Arabia, but was arrested in that country and kept for two years in captivity. He escaped and after many adventures reached Calcutta and was entertained at a public dinner. He became Paymaster-General to the East India Company and made a second fortune, with which he found his way to Baltimore, which he afterwards represented in the Legislature of Maryland, becoming Colonel of the Maryland Militia. One of his grandsons, returning to the Truagh Castle estates, rose to high rank in the British Army, as General Sir Charles Routledge O'Donnell, K.C.B.

Patrick O'Donnell of Chicago, the most eloquent lawyer in the United States, showed the grit of his race by meeting and defeating the anti-Catholic organisation known as the Ku-Klux-Klan in the

Patrick O'Donnell, of Chicago.

States of the Middle West. He was offered an Ambassadorship by President Harding, but refused it in order to carry on his attack on bigotry, and won a lasting success. Though undoubtedly sprung from the Donegal nobility, an ancestor being an officer at the battle of Kinsale, his family had clung to the profession of farming till his legal mind and eloquence opened up another career.

A Great Lawyer.

My only brother, Mr. Frank Hugh O'Donnell, —*O! et præsidium et dulce decus meum,*—who died in November, 1916, is forgotten probably by the majority of Irishmen, but his work remains. He was Member of Parliament for Galway and Dungarvan for about ten years, and Sir Henry W. Lucy, one of the keenest of political observers, describes in *Parliamentary Reminiscences* his entry into public life in these words : " Amongst the group of Irishmen, who flooded the Parliament of 1874-80 with strange characters and dominated it with new manners, the most brilliant was Frank Hugh O'Donnell, M.P. for Dungarvan. Cultivated in a measure far beyond the average of his compatriots, gifted with Parliamentary instinct, polished wit, and a ready tongue, Mr. O'Donnell early won a position as the most formidable of the insurgent body. It was he who devised the subtle system of obstructing Parliamentary business."

"The Most Brilliant."

After his death, the Rt. Honble. T. P. O'Connor, M.P., wrote in the *Daily Telegraph* :

" No man began life with a greater determination

to succeed and more endowed with many of the gifts that make for success. He loved power; he loved leadership; he loved to live in the eyes of men; and he had an absolute and inflexible self-confidence. There were resemblances between his temperament and that of young Disraeli. He was a dandy in his youth; he was good looking; he had a presence and he courted observation. He was equally notable as an athlete."

Success Impossible

Mr. O'Donnell left the House of Commons because he foresaw that success was impossible, for himself or for the Irish Party. For ten years he had all the joys of being the darling of Home Rule platforms, but he had come to understand that, with Parnell as leader, nothing more ennobling than the Kilmainham Treaty lay in the future. He was sickened by the futilities and meannesses and worse underlying the Parnell *régime*.

Mr. O'Connor continues: "His ambition was apparently justified by his great gifts. He was a splendid student and he had tremendous industry, a powerful memory, and an insatiable appetite for information. He had, in fact, an extraordinarily well-equipped mind. He knew several languages. He read French, Italian, and German almost as easily as English, an accomplishment that proved his best weapon for entering journalism in later life. Wherever he found himself he would be surrounded by stacks of books. He talked exceedingly well. He was a writer of extraordinary readiness and

Great Gifts and World-wide Knowledge

versatility." He might have been the corner
stone of Irish regeneration, but he was in advance
of his time and was defeated by the squalid intrigues
of men, whose patriotism bowed prone before the
backstairs of an English political party. He also
knew what Parnell's private life was and rejected
such companionship.

" O'Donnell undoubtedly was a great Parliamentary figure, and in knowledge and versatility
he was far beyond Parnell. He had
a world-wide knowledge of politics ; **"A Great Parliamentary Figure "**
he was ready, resourceful, exhaust-
less in speech and brilliant in phrase-making.
His speeches, obstructive though they were, remained brilliant, amusing, and though they
exasperated, they also interested the House. Now
and then he startled the House with some striking
phrase. He would speak of a City alderman
who interrupted him as guilty of ' turtle-fed
boorishness.' If anything were necessary to
increase the white rage which O'Donnell often
produced in the House by his speeches it was
supplied by his manner. Partly by temperament,
partly by calculation, he cultivated a maddening
superciliousness." He sincerely despised the
baseness of politics and had an intense contempt
for both Parties, Conservatives and Liberal, for
their maintaining or winking at religious oppression in Ulster.

" His wide knowledge of politics in all parts of
the world supplied to the less inventive and less
stored minds of Parnell and Biggar the material

for obstruction. It was he who planned the alliance with the advocates of the Boers that produced the first of the prolonged **"The Spokesman of Discontent."** all-night sittings. It was his fertile mind that first saw in the agitation for the abolition of flogging in the Army not merely a great reform, but a means of prolonging discussion of the Mutiny Bill practically over a whole wasted and disastrous session.[1] He found suitable material in the aspirations of many important leaders of Indian thought for an enlargement of native participation in the government of our great Dependency, and he did succeed in bringing together a very representative and powerful conference of Indian magnates in London,—which may have been the spiritual root of many of the modern movements in India to-day. His favourite theory was that the Irish Party should make itself the spokesman of the discontent of all the other races in the Empire."

It is typical of the degenerate party that Parnell had emasculated that Mr. O'Connor had no word of regret for the loss of its most **The Prophet of Sinn Fein.** effective, scholarly and gifted member, " a great Parliamentary figure." He was an obstacle to its degradation and made

[1] In an article of the 12th May, 1910, the *Law Times*, the leading organ of the legal profession in England, described how " Mr. O'Donnell and his party during three months obstructed and obstructed till the flogging clauses were killed. It was a great humanitarian battle and a great achievement. He made the Army of the Empire an honourable profession."

no attempt to find an Irish seat in after years.
He was busy on his life's real work, the instilling
into the minds of the Irish people that they must
rely on themselves in Ireland—*Sinn Fein*—and
not pin their faith " to English Radicals like
Parnell and O'Connor in a foreign assembly."

Before attacking the Parliamentary side of the
Irish ulcer my brother had to clear the way by
an assault on the political side of
his beloved Church. Years before **Devastating Books.**
it had been driven into his unwilling
mind that the Catholic hierarchy in Ireland had
given hostages to Dublin Castle by subordinating
everything to securing the control and the funds
of education. No sacrifice was too great to make
in order to make sure of these advantages. Mr.
O'Donnell produced in 1903 and 1908 two absolutely devastating books. *The Ruin of Education
in Ireland* and *Paraquay on Shannon,*—" The price
of a political priesthood." Three editions of the
first were soon scattered throughout every corner
of Ireland and their effect was monumental. Even
the priests, certainly the younger ones, began to
feel that something was very wrong and the
study of the Irish language and of Irish history,
which had been practically excluded from the
Clerical Schools, gave a new and ardent vigour
to the drooping spirits of Irish Nationalism. Whilst
the so-called Irish Party was hobnobbing with
the Treasury Bench, Frank Hugh was laying
the foundations of a new era. *Paraquay on
Shannon* carried the criticism of the nation-killing

methods of the Catholic hierarchy a step farther and gave strength to the body of young patriots, who were grouping themselves round Arthur Griffith, for whom my brother maintained a warm affection to his dying day, visiting him in prison and helping him with an almost world-wide experience.

Mr. O'Donnell's main work, however, remained to be done, and in 1910 he published *The History of the Irish Parliamentary Party*, which immediately had an enormous success. A chorus of admiration from almost every journal **" An Extraordinary Book."** welcomed its appearance. The *Nineteenth Century* declared that : " This book is not unworthy of the expectation with which it was awaited. . . . It helps us as no previously published book helps us "—and the *Spectator* recognized that :

" Mr. O'Donnell has given us a book of singular interest."

The *Outlook*, the organ of young Conservatism, added :

" Mr. F. H. O'Donnell has three of the qualities required in a historian of his own times : a good memory, a lively style, and a conscientious disregard for other people's feelings. . . . A man of long lineage and sensitive culture . . . he has produced a huge work full of good things in the way of entertainment, observation, and suggestion. A witty, candid, and interesting work."

I add a few other appreciations :

The *St. James's Gazette*.—" Brilliantly written,

full of real Irish wit, humour, and eloquence, spark-
ling with epigram, richly coloured with anecdote,
Mr. O'Donnell's history insists on being read carefully through the whole of its thousand pages."

The *Daily Mail*—" It is a merciless indictment
of the Irish Parliamentary Party by one who
himself was among the Irish ' Old Guard ' . . .
Mr. O'Donnell writes well ; he can use words
like a whip lash ; and much of his story is of the
highest historical and political interest."

Pall Mall Gazette—" Irish politics have so long
stamped themselves upon the English mind as an
unsavoury mixture of sentiment, sordidness, and
sensation that the writer, who is capable of giving
to the story something of historical dignity and
consecutive interest, is capable of a good deal.
To say that he writes picturesquely and strongly
will seem superfluous to those acquainted with
his *Paraquay on Shannon.*"

The *Daily News*—" A very interesting book.
. . . Mr. O'Donnell is admittedly one of the most
brilliant men who have entered Irish Parliamentary
politics during the past forty years. . . . Very
valuable, too, is Mr. O'Donnell's reminder of
the inclination of many of the Irish gentry to
take part in national politics till the agrarian
agitation put an almost impassable barrier between
them and the people."

The *Irish Times*, the organ of Irish Protestantism.
—" Messrs. Longmans, Green & Co. publish to-day
a book which will be read with feelings of regret
and even shame and humiliation wherever the

The Irish Future

English tongue is spoken. . . . The Englishman will find his nation convicted of political blundering of the grossest description. The Nationalist will read Mr. O'Donnell's disclosures with the most acute pain. His work might almost be called ' the decline and fall of the Home Rule movement.' It is a tremendous indictment of the policy of Parnell."

The *Westminster Gazette*, the organ of English Liberalism.—" Mr. O'Donnell's *extraordinary book* may be read with profit by a few politicians of all parties. They will, most of them, read something in it which their best friends are studiously con-cealing from them, and which, by way of discipline, it is good for them to read and think over. . . . This book is a remarkable achievement. . . . Nothing could be finer than his criticism of the policy of the Act of Union, which, whatever its merits, deprived the Irish gentry of any chance of a career in their own country, and widened the gulf which separated them from the tenant occupiers of the soil. The mismanagement of the British Government at the time of the great famine of 1846-7 is exposed in language worthy of the appalling incapacity then displayed by the rulers of Ireland. The author has, it is true, gone over beaten ground in this part of his narrative, as every one knows who has read Disraeli's *Life of Lord George Bentinck* or Father O'Rourke's *History of the Great Famine*, or the writings of that great master of English prose, John Mitchel ; but he is not excelled by the literary grace of the first, or the sorrowful painstakingness of the second, or the nervous vigour of the last.

The Irish Future

So, too, he makes a just contribution to history in showing that the policy of Obstruction was not mere vindictiveness."

This book killed the ridiculous Parnellite cult and made straight the ways of true Irish National-ism. It did more. It recognised the patriotism of Protestant Irishmen **"God Save England."** and showed how, landowners as they largely were, they had been driven into the anti-Irish camp by the communist teaching of Parnell and Michael Davitt. It breathed not one word against any Englishman, except the party organisers, who made use of Orange bigotry for the evil ends of the worst English Toryism. Mr. O'Donnell loved the English people,—as I venture to say I do,—and regarded " God save England " as righteous an aspiration as " God save Ireland." His policy was, as mine is, simply " Repeal of the Union," with representation in the Imperial Parliament in proportion to population.

Mr. T. P. O'Connor, who is an acute observer, accurately estimated one of the chief objects that my brother worked for in the House of Commons, when he wrote, " His **"Indian Magnates."** favourite theory was that the Irish Party should make itself the spokesman of the discontent of all the other races in the Empire," and he instanced especially his " bringing together a very representative and powerful conference of Indian magnates in London, which may have been the spiritual root of many of the modern movements in India to-day." Mr. O'Connor is

261

The Irish Future

quite right. Mr. O'Donnell's work has lived and will go on living long after Parnellism is forgotten.

Mr. O'Donnell wrote much very effective poetry and laboured to keep alive the memory of ancient Ireland. In his *Message of the Masters* he drew a picture of her clans.

Ancient Ireland.

See Shan the King comes riding, proud Ulster's
    proudest knight,
In royal robe of saffron, on his war horse white;
With Kildare's Silken Thomas, who flung too soon
    the sword,
That might have cut our bondage, on Tudor's
    council board;
O'Carrol, Prince of Ely, the lion in the way;
And Battleaxe MacSwiney, from Fanad's mountains
    grey.

O'More, our glorious Rury, who chased the Planter
    Foe,
O'More who planned the rising that brought us
    Owen Roe;
O'Gara, bounteous giver to annalist and bard,
To latest age of ages that name let Ireland
    guard;
O'Kelly of Hy Many, O'Farrel, Longford's pride,
And many a bold MacKenna, who far from Oriel died.

O'Kennedy of Ormond, O'Ryan of Idrone,
O'Cahan of Tir Cahan, the battler of Tyrone;
O'Felan, Lord of Decies, O'Toole of true Imayle,
O'Duffies and O'Mearas, who kept the golden Vale.

The Irish Future

O'Hanlons, Chiefs of Orior, with Remy's Raparees ;
When Remy's men are riding, how fast the planter
flees !

MacCann of broad Clanbrasil, MacManus of Loch
Erne,
MacGrath, the courtly champion, the Lord of
Templecarne ;
MacGee, who held the Island, MacGinnis of
Iveagh,
MacLoghlin and O'Connellan, the wardens of Loch
Neagh ;

MacMahon, Lord of Truagh, MacDonnel of the
Glens,
MacDaid, the Oakgrove's Ranger, who smoked
the Robbers' dens,
O'Hurley, Cashel's Martyr, whom Saxon tortures
slew,
And Dublin's sainted Lawrence, Bishop and Soldier,
too ;

O'Malley of the Waters, O'Daly of the Wood ;
O'Doherty's Sir Cahir, whose dawn was drowned
in blood ;
O'Dwyer of the Mountain, O'Driscol of the Shore ;
O'Flaherty the Fearless, where Aran's surges roar.

MacGuire of fair Fermanagh by Dunboy's Chieftain
runs,
And Sarsfield shouts with passion, as when he broke
the guns.

The Irish Future

With Desmond's last Fitzgerald is high MacCarthy
    Mor,
And Glemmalure's O'Byrne strides up to join the
    Four.

Another very effective method was adopted by
Mr. O'Donnell to reach Irish opinion. He was
a man of complete leisure, who could
Dark Rosaleen. devote the whole of his time to
advancing the cause of what was to
him "Holy Ireland, Ever Dear." His was the
enthusiasm and energy that could move mount-
tains. He had a list of leading and influential
men made out for every county in Ireland and,
with the help of a very capable Scotch Secretary,
poured out by means of private letters a ceaseless
criticism of the feckless gentlemen who called
themselves the Nationalist Party. He also taught
them what Irish History really was and meant.
"Resurgam" was the motto he imagined for his
Dark Rosaleen.

> " The Erne at its highest flood
> I dashed across unseen.
> There was lightning in my blood,
>   Red lightning lightened through my blood,
>   My Dark Rosaleen."

Frank Hugh O'Donnell worked unseen, seeking
neither notoriety nor reward, for the red lightning
of a supreme patriotism coursed through his
veins.

The Irish Future

I can notice only very shortly his work for Ireland on the Continent. Soon after his arrival in London, he was so fortunate as to win the friendships of Cardinal **" The Sister of Columbia. "** Manning, who regarded him with affection till his death, and of the Duc de Broglie, the French Ambassador. Aided by introductions from them, he formed a wide circle of acquaintances amongst statesmen in Catholic countries and, with his linguistic attainments, told the story of Ireland in journals so dissimilar as the *Republique* of Paris and the *Neue Freie Presse* of Vienna. After he left Parliament he extended his interests and in Berlin, Petersburg and New York continued his patriotic work. Claiming, as he did, to be eleventh in lineal descent from Roderick O'Donnell, last Earl of Tyrconnell by Margarita O'Neil, daughter of the last Earl of Tyrone, he sought and found in many a Continental home the heirs and descendants of the ancient Irish nobility, who fled from the old country after the repudiation of the Treaty of Limerick by the British Government. He poured contempt on their upstart and cruel successors, " The sireless Saxon squatters, Clan London's loutish lords." Mr. J. A. Froude, in his *English in Ireland*, records how this undesirable gentry was regarded, even by Englishmen, as " men of desperate fortunes, the scum of their nation that come over with the armies." Sir Henry Sidney, whom Queen Elizabeth had specially sent as Lord Deputy, wrote of the Pale or English counties as " overwhelmed by

The Irish Future

vagabonds " from across the Irish Sea. Unhappy
Ireland !

Frank Hugh O'Donnell's career might well be a
beacon light to the young men and women of
New Ireland. The miseries and degradations of
recent years will pass away and, lit by the memories
of the proud centuries, " e'er her faithless sons
betrayed her," Ireland will take her place as " The
Sister of Columbia, the Peer of any Nation in the
World."